HOSPITALITY
Recipes Full of Love

PRESENTED BY THE AUXILIARY OF SHEPHERD CENTER

SHEPHERD CENTER
A Catastrophic Care Hospital
Atlanta, Georgia

Special thanks to the Shepherd Center Foundation
and the Shepherd Center Public Relations Department
for their outstanding support of this Auxiliary Cookbook.

Cookbook Design courtesy of Jones Design Group, Atlanta, Georgia

ISBN# 0-9785652-0-7

First Printing 3000 copies 2006

WIMMER
COOKBOOKS

A CONSOLIDATED GRAPHICS COMPANY

800.548.2537   wimmerco.com

In the beginning…

Shepherd Center began with the one phone call no parent ever wants; the one call which is thereafter etched in your mind. After graduation from the University of Georgia, our son, James, was paralyzed in a body surfing accident in Brazil in 1973. In critical condition and on a ventilator, James remained in Rio for six weeks with his family at his bedside. We finally arranged for a U.S. Air Force Medevac flight which brought us all to Atlanta. James continued to lose ground for three months in an Atlanta hospital. We then transferred him to a facility in Denver which specialized in spinal cord injuries. James was down to 87 pounds but slowly began to make progress. His injury was incomplete so return of function and sensation began. He walked out five months later with a leg brace and a crutch.

After returning home, he and other Atlantans who had been treated in Colorado believed a spinal cord unit should be in Atlanta and said, "Why don't we start something?" The "we" suddenly became us. Enlisting Dr. David Apple, Jr. as medical director was a key step. The Shepherd Spinal Center opened in 1975 with six beds. They quickly filled and so did a waiting list.

Specialty rehabilitation hospitals are very different from general hospitals and so approach the patient differently. Our staff is committed to creating the optimum level of care and service through individualized patient programs, all in an atmosphere of support and respect. As our reputation has spread, thousands of people have benefited from this model of care. With an intensive care unit, acute care and day program, patients with spinal injuries are offered a continuum of care, utilizing our second campus for their day program. Shepherd is proud to be the largest Multiple Sclerosis Center in the Southeast.

The staff continues to reach for the stars to help patients rebuild their lives with hope, dignity and independence, advocating for their full inclusion in all aspects of community life. Our family is so grateful to have been able to play a part in delivering hope to those who have been so catastrophically injured.

Now, wear your seat belts and enjoy selecting and preparing a delicious recipe from this book.

Alana Shepherd

Alana Shepherd
Secretary
Board of Directors

RECIPE CONTRIBUTORS

Antonio Abizanda
Dot Addison
Helen Aderhold
Cookie Aftergut
Alison Akard
Mary Alice Alexander
Zana Allen
Liz Anderson
Jan Andrews
Jane Apple
Deborah Ashendorf
Joane Askins
Marion Atkins
Marion Taulman Bales
Neale Bearden
Marianne Beasley
Elaine Bennett
Eleanor Bernhardt
Betty Besten
Margaret Bethea
Suzanne Bible
Marcia Bourne
Polly Bowman
Robert O. Breitling Jr.
Joan Brown
Jan Buchanan
Angela Buckley
Maryann Busby
Ann Caldwell
Aline Callahan
Park Callahan

Bonnie Capsuto
Rosalynn Carter
Marilyn Cates
Sara Chapman
Helen Christiansen
Mary Cindrus
Dee Claflin
Sarah Clarke
Roni Cochran
Denise Cohen
Millie Coleman
Alida Coles
Cathy Compton
Ansley Conner
Peggy Conner
Tony Conway
Betsy Cozine
Charles Craig
Carol Crichton
Jean Crichton
Joyce Crichton
Debi Cziok
Bob Dalton
Carol Dew
Patti Dimond
Martha Dinos
Jim Dodgson
Alyson Boyea Doherty
Faye Donaldson
Merrie Beth Donehew
Gary Donlick

Jane Elias
Bev Ellithorp
Ginny Ellithorp
John Ellithorp
Sergio Favalli
Barbara Flowers
Cheryl Foos
Betsy Fox
Sue Freeman
Jeannine Freer
Jackie Fryer
Jerry Gaines
Joseph Geonczy
Mary Gilbreath
Patty Golub
Carol Goodman
Sarah Goodman
Debbie Goot
Kathy Grant
Dolores Greene
Rhette Greenlees
Jean Gregory
Rachelle Grigor
Debbie Gross
Becca Harrell
Zuma Harris
Hope Harrison
Sam Harrison
Mary Hataway
Lynn Hatch
Shirley Heerman

Julie Henderson
Hallie Henrickson
Milt Hibbard
Louise Hicks
Robert Holley
Christophe Holmes
Ron Horgan
Mary Frances Howard
Mary Kay Howard
Mary Sue Howard
Bibba Hurst
Edna Mae Husley
Bev Hynes
Florence Inman
Lucy Inman
Suzanne Inman
Dianne Isakson
Gail Johnson
Andrea Johnson
Kathy Johnson
Christophe Joignant
Carol Jones
Katharine Jones
Nancy Jungman
Martha Jo Katz
Neil Kelley
Ward Kelly
Gayle Kennedy
Bobbie Ann Kirkland
Eula Kirkland
Betty Kreimer

We wish to thank our many friends in the North, East, South and West who have submitted their special recipes. Those not used, due to limitation of space, are being carefully saved. Who knows, there may be a Volume II some day.

Gloria Landreth
Alice Lanier
Joanne LeCraw
Ann Levin
Carol Lindsey
Mattie Lisenby
Sharon Lufkin
David Lundy
Candy Lusby
Becky Maddox
Billie Claire Mangum
Nita Manuel
Bart Marks
Mary Massey
Nancy McClannan
Connie McClellan
Dianne McKnight
Dean Melcher
Beverly Mitchell
Julie Isakson Mitchell
Pat Monaco
Nancy Montgomery
Annelle Moore
Linda Morris
Rena Morrison
Betty Munford
Virginia Murphy
Sandra Mysen
Elizabeth Neal
Sary Newman
Valeria Burnett Orr

Paul Pate
Diana Patterson
Neville Pearson
Pamela Penn
Cherri Penton
Mary Perdue
Triff Phillips
Charles Pottinger lll
Mary Pottinger
Connie Preston
Joyce Preston
Lois Puckett
Linda Putnam
Jutta Putter
Loredana Reuter
Nancy Ricker
Louise Riddle
Martha Lou Riddle
June Rose
Marty Rosenfield
Jan Ruane
Pamela Ruhland
Fran Russell
Louis Russo
Mickey Sachs
Frances Sasser
Scott Serpas
Carol Sharkey
Deborah Sharkey
Kevin Sharkey
Doris Shelton

Alana Shepherd
Linda and James Shepherd
Mary Ellen Sherman
Mary Ann Sikes
Peggy Slotin
Claire Smith
Barbara Smith
Andrew Snow
Sallie Snow
Judy Spalding
Erna Spears
Elizabeth Spiegel
Karen Spiegel
Beth St. Jean
Carol Stephens
Mary Stephens
Marian Stevens
Kathleen Stichnot
Cile Stockhausen
Gloria Stone
Kate Stradtman
Julia Hurd Strong
Karen Sturm
Linda Lou Sumlin
Janet Sunshine
Beth Taquechel
Erinn Tatom
Sharon Tatom
Susan Taulman
The Swag

Katie Thomas
Carol Thompson
Dorothy Thrower
Midge Tracy
Ann Trufant
Jane Ulicny
Patrick VanBiesen
Ruth Vaught
Joan Ventresca
Stacie Waddell
Cecilia Waddey
Kevin Walker
Marty Wallace
Stacie Wallace
Tracey Wallace
Parker Watkins
June Weitnauer
Hilary White
Elspeth Willcoxon
Ann Williams
Cathy Williams
Patricia Williams
Pauline Willis
Lanie Joan Wilson
Sally Wintheiser
Ginny Wolf
Hortense Wolf
Lynne Yancey
Jay Yarbrough
Maggie Young

Auxiliary President 2005 - 2006
Mary Kay Howard

Chairman, Editor in Chief
Florence Inman

Assistant Chairman (Publicity)
Beverly Mitchell

Chairman Marketing and Sales
Lois Puckett

**Assistant Chairman
Marketing and Sales**
Faye Donaldson

Marilyn Cates
Cathy Compton
Betsy Cozine
Martha Dinos
Lucy Inman
Triff Phillips

Chairman Typing and Coding
Debbie Goot

Bonnie Capsuto
Mary Sue Howard

Business Manager
Bonnie Capsuto

Order Processing
Mary Kay Howard

**Chairman Recipe Collecting
and Testing**
Carol Sharkey

Testers
Cookie Aftergut
Deborah Ashendorf
Joane Askins
Marian Atkins

Eleanor Bernhardt
Margaret Bethea
Polly Bowman
Linda Bridges
Mardee Brooks
Marla Brooks
Angela Buckley
Bonnie Capsuto
Marilyn Cates
Sara Chapman
Jen Cloud
Cathy Compton
Gracia Conn
Ansley Conner
Peggy Conner
Betsy Cozine
Debi Cziok
Leah Dennis
Nancy Dilly
Martha Dinos
Faye Donaldson
Ashley Felton
Linda Fraser
Jeannine Freer
Candice Gibson
Kimbrough Gibson
Ina Gill
Mary Gilbreath
Maryann Gillespie
Debbie Goot
Rhette Greenlees
Mary Frances Howard
Mary Kay Howard
Mary Sue Howard
Pam Howard
Greer Hughes
Florence Inman
Andrea Johnson

Molly Lanier
Elena Leonard
David Lundy
Bart Marks
Beverly Mitchell
Julie Isakson Mitchell
Rena Morrison
Heather Nash
Carol Olsen
Gene Rowe
Carol Sharkey
Kevin Sharkey
Doris Shelton
Barbara Smith
Betty Smith
Courtney Smith
Gloria Stone
Catherine Sweat
Beth Taquechel
Susan Taulman
Betty Teem
Midge Tracy
Jane Ulicny
Sandy Unruh
Elizabeth Waddey
Ginny Wolf
Hortense Wolf

Proof Reading
Jeannine Freer and
Katharine Jones,
Co-Chairmen

Pat Harrell
Shirley Heermann
Janet Johnson
Doris Shelton
Joan Sites
Betty Teem
Betty Webster

Mission Statement

To provide on-going financial support for Shepherd Center Auxiliary's patient related programs and to increase awareness of Shepherd Center as a catastrophic care hospital.

Table of Contents

HOSPITALITY ♥ Recipes Full of Love

Patient Stories

Marshall Hamilton's Story

In 2000, Marshall Hamilton was on his way to go whitewater rafting with two friends when the driver of the car they were in fell asleep and the car went down an embankment. The two friends walked away from the accident unhurt, but Marshall wasn't as lucky — he had sustained a paralyzing spinal cord injury. Marshall was transported by helicopter to a Chattanooga hospital and later taken on a stretcher by ambulance to Shepherd Center where he began his recovery in the spinal cord injury unit. After weeks of rehabilitation, Marshall was able to walk with the assistance of a leg brace and walking cane, which he continues to use today. Since then, he has returned to Shepherd Center to serve as a volunteer, which includes visiting and talking with patients as part of Shepherd's peer support program. "Sometimes it is easier for a patient to hear what has to be said from me rather than from a therapist," he says. Marshall is also involved in Shepherd Center's sports team, including the quad rugby team, Shepherd Smash. The team plays regionally and in competitions across the nation. The players share a unique camaraderie. "Everyone on the team has had an injury," he said. "We are kind of like a family. Shepherd is my Rock. I love this place."

Marshall Hamilton

Parker King's Story

Parker King was 17 when he was injured as a pedestrian who was struck by a pickup truck. He sustained numerous injuries, including a brain injury. After receiving treatment at three hospitals, he was moved to Shepherd Center to begin months of therapy to restore his brain and mental functions. Today, looking back on his recovery, Parker says his therapists knew when to push and when to hold back with love and care. Along the way, he said, he slowly but steadily gained more and more function and his will to live and get better. After his discharge from Shepherd Center, Parker returned to high school and graduated. He took time to travel the world before returning to the U.S. to begin college - something his family never thought would be possible just after the accident happened. "All of us are in so many ways better people than before Parker's accident," said Parker's mom, Betty. "I serve on a Shepherd Foundation Board; it's so great to give back. Three factors played a part in Parker's success…the Man up there, Shepherd and Parker's powerful will."

Betty King

Bob Dalton's Story

Bob Dalton was struck by a drunk driver in 1995 and sustained severe head injuries as a result of the accident. He was admitted to the brain injury unit at Shepherd Center while he was still in a coma. As he emerged from the coma, Bob began rehabilitation and after several months of hard work, he was able to go back home. Bob had planned to return to work, but unfortunately that wasn't an option. So he decided to become a volunteer. Initially Bob's wife, Angie, drove him to Shepherd Center where his volunteer duties included escorting patients to the cafeteria for lunch. He now drives himself to Shepherd and makes himself available whenever he's needed as a volunteer. At Shepherd Center's 2004 Independent Volunteer Awards Ceremony, Bob received a standing ovation. Whenever anyone asks him why he spends so much time volunteering, his answer is always the same: "I love this place, I love everybody here and I love coming down here to help. I'll do anything I can to help Shepherd Center."

Bob's Tropical Fruit

2	pints strawberries	2	8-ounce containers frozen nondairy whipped topping
5	kiwi		
4	8¼-ounce cans Mandarin oranges, drained		

Wash strawberries and cut to preferred size; peel and slice kiwi. In large glass bowl, place layer of Mandarin oranges; then add layer of whipped topping. Add layer of strawberries and then another layer of whipped topping. Place slices of kiwi on top.

Bob has contributed over 3,275 volunteer hours to Shepherd. He makes this dessert for patients, staff, other volunteers and family members by request several times a year. They all love it.

Bob Dalton, Atlanta, GA

Carol Olsen's Story

Carol Olsen was a BellSouth manager in Atlanta. In 2001, in anticipation of a potential labor strike, management employees trained to perform jobs normally done by non-management employees. Carol was asked to climb a telephone pole. She made it to the top, but as she came down, she fell. She was admitted to Shepherd Center with a dual-diagnosis injury. She had sustained both a brain injury and a spinal cord injury. Carol does not remember much about her first four weeks at Shepherd. Her first clear memory is that of lying on a mat in the therapy gym and feeling the cold nose of a Chocolate Lab named Buster. "Buster came up on the mat and gently waited for me to touch him. That was the day my rehab really began." Throughout her stay at Shepherd, Carol looked forward to the visits from Buster and his friends, human and canine. Carol returned to BellSouth and walks with a cane.

Carol J Olsen

Alyson Doherty's Story

Alyson Doherty's stay at Shepherd Center's Acquired Brain Injury unit began after being transferred from another hospital following a car accident. Alyson doesn't remember arriving at Shepherd Center, but she does recall the support she received while she was there. "I remember being pushed, pulled, carried, praised, and encouraged, as well as the wonderful patience of all the staff," she says. "I hated having to go through it all, and there were so many times I could have given up, but I am a fighter and Shepherd Center encourages and inspires fighters. They kept reminding me over and over how important my hard work was and how I really was making progress — tiny advances every day that all added up over my two-month-stay and allowed me to walk out on my own two feet. I am married now to the wonderful guy who saw me through those long, hard months and years of recovery. Thank you, God, Shepherd, Dr. Leslie, ABI staff, Rehab and my supportive family."

Alyson Boyea Doherty

Potatoes Romanoff

12	medium red potatoes	½	cup diced onions
2	cups cottage cheese		salt and pepper to taste
1	8-ounce carton sour cream		grated Cheddar cheese to cover

Cook potatoes in skins until soft but firm enough to slice or dice; cool and slice or dice. Fold in cottage cheese, sour cream, onion, salt and pepper. Spoon into greased baking dish and top with grated cheese. Bake in preheated 350 degree oven for 45 minutes.

Put cheese on right before baking or potatoes will turn dark.

Alyson Boyea Doherty, Woburn, MA

Carol Crisco's Story

Carol Crisco says that no matter how you get to Shepherd Center, you arrive with a broken body and sometimes a broken heart. Carol's injury occurred as the result of an elective surgery, which caused paralysis in her legs. While at Shepherd Center, one of Carol's most moving experiences was being fitted for a wheelchair. "I could have filled all of Atlanta with my tears and maybe I did," she says. "But tears were not going to get me back on my feet. So the hard work began. Learning to walk again was the hardest thing I have ever done in my life." One day, while on a hospital outing to a restaurant, Carol met a fellow patient who was paralyzed in a skiing accident. She recalls: "I was sitting in my wheelchair tapping my feet on the footrest, and the young man looked at me and said, 'Wow, you can move your ankles?!' That put a great many things in perspective for me." At the end of her stay, Carol walked out of Shepherd Center. One footnote she likes to share: "Six years after leaving Shepherd Center, at age 40, Miracle Max was born. The three of us enjoy walking together, hand in hand, whenever we can."

Carol P. Crisco

Bread and Breakfast

HOSPITALITY

Pineapple Muffins

½   cup sugar
⅓   cup shortening
⅓   cup honey
2   eggs
1⅓   cups all-bran
1⅓   cups flour
2   teaspoons baking soda
½   teaspoon salt
1   cup evaporated milk
1   cup crushed pineapple, well drained

Cream together sugar, shortening and honey. Add eggs, all-bran, flour, soda, salt, milk and pineapple and mix lightly. Fill greased muffin pan cups ⅓ full. Bake in preheated 350 degree oven for 25 minutes.

Makes 18 muffins

Cover the pan with wax paper and store in refrigerator overnight to bake up fresh in the morning.

"They teach you so many things at Shepherd Center. You end up doing things you never thought you could."

Michael Padgett,
former SCI patient

Raisin Bran Muffins

5   cups flour
3   cups sugar
5   teaspoons baking soda
1½   teaspoons salt
1   15-ounce box raisin bran cereal
4   cups buttermilk
1   cup vegetable oil
4   eggs, beaten

Blend flour, sugar, soda and salt in large mixing bowl. Stir in cereal; add buttermilk, oil and eggs and blend until dry ingredients are moistened. Do not stir batter again. Fill greased muffin pan ⅔ full and bake in preheated 400 degree oven for 15 to 20 minutes.

Batter may be covered and stored in a non-metal bowl in the refrigerator up to six weeks.

Eula Kirkland, Rome, GA

Strawberry Shortcake Muffins

2	cups flour
½	cup sugar, divided
2	teaspoons baking powder
½	teaspoon salt
1	cup milk
1	egg, slightly beaten
¼	cup melted butter
15	strawberries, sliced

Combine flour, ¼ cup sugar, baking powder and salt in large bowl. Stir in milk, egg and butter, stirring only enough to dampen all flour; batter will not be smooth. Spoon into buttered muffin cups, filling each about ⅔ full. Press strawberry slices into batter, pointed side up. Sprinkle each muffin with remaining sugar. Bake in preheated 425 degree oven until golden, 15 to 18 minutes.

Makes 1 dozen

Debbie Goot, Atlanta, GA

Banana Nut Bread

½	cup butter or margarine, softened
1	cup sugar
2	eggs, beaten
3	ripe bananas, mashed
2	cups flour
1	teaspoon baking soda
	pinch of salt
1	cup chopped pecans or almonds
1	teaspoon vanilla extract

Cream butter and sugar until light and fluffy. Add eggs and bananas and mix well. Combine flour, soda and salt; stir into banana mixture until all ingredients are moistened. Stir in nuts and vanilla. Spoon batter into greased 9x5x3 inch loaf pan and bake in preheated 250 degree oven for 1½ hours or until bread tests done.

Makes 1 loaf

Roni Cochran, Anderson, SC

Uncle Milt's Mayonnaise Muffins

2	cups self-rising flour
1	cup milk
½	cup mayonnaise
1	tablespoon sugar

Mix together flour, milk, mayonnaise and sugar and put into well greased muffin tin. Bake in preheated 425 degree oven until lightly browned, about 10 minutes.

Makes 1 dozen

Mamie Anthony's recipe from the MVPC Blue Cookbook. Now served at Mt. Vernon Village under the name "Uncle Milt's Muffins."

Milt Hubbard,
Atlanta, GA

Coconut Bread

1	cup butter, softened
2	cups sugar
6	eggs
1	12-ounce box vanilla wafers, crushed
1	7-ounce package flaked coconut
1	cup chopped nuts

Cream butter and sugar. Add eggs, one at a time, and mix well. Add crumbs, coconut and nuts. Spoon into two greased and floured loaf pans and bake in preheated 350 degree oven for 1 hour.

Makes 1 loaf

Judy Spalding, Cumming, GA

Pumpkin Bread

2⅔	cups sugar
1	cup shortening
4	eggs
3⅓	cups flour
1	teaspoon baking powder
2	teaspoons baking soda
1	14-ounce can solid pumpkin
1½	teaspoons salt
1	teaspoon cinnamon
½	teaspoon cloves

Cream sugar and shortening. Add eggs, flour, baking powder, soda, pumpkin, salt, cinnamon and cloves. Stir until well mixed. Pour into 2 greased and floured loaf pans and bake in preheated 350 degree oven for 1 hour.

Makes 2 loaves

Katie Thomas, Atlanta, GA

Orange Marmalade Marble Loaf

1	3-ounce package cream cheese, softened
¼	cup orange marmalade
1	16½-ounce package date quick bread mix
1	cup milk
1	tablespoon oil
1	egg

In small bowl, blend cream cheese and orange marmalade; set aside. In large bowl, combine bread mix, milk, oil and egg; stir 50 to 75 strokes until dry particles are moistened. Pour half of batter into greased and floured 8x4 inch loaf pan. Pour cream cheese mixture over batter. Pour remaining batter over cream cheese mixture. To marble, pull knife through batter in wide curves. Bake in preheated 350 degree oven for 65 to 75 minutes or until golden brown. Cool 15 minutes; remove from pan. Cool completely on wire rack. Wrap tightly; store in refrigerator.

Makes 1 loaf

Nut quick bread mix can be substituted. Add 1 additional tablespoon oil to the recipe above.

A 9x5 inch loaf pan can be substituted; grease and flour bottom only. Bake 55 to 65 minutes or until golden brown.

Carol Sharkey, Atlanta, GA

Crispy Cornsticks

1	cup cornmeal
½	cup flour
2½	teaspoons baking powder
½	teaspoon salt
⅛	teaspoon baking soda
1	teaspoon sugar
2	eggs
1	cup buttermilk
2	tablespoons oil

Heavily grease cornstick pans and place in preheated 450 degree oven to heat. Mix cornmeal, flour, baking powder, salt, soda and sugar. Beat eggs with milk and oil; add to dry ingredients and mix until smooth. Pour into hot cornstick pans and bake until brown.

Millie Coleman, Atlanta, GA

Buttermilk Biscuits

2	cups flour
2	teaspoons baking powder
1	teaspoon sugar
½	teaspoon salt
¼	cup plus 1 tablespoon shortening
½	teaspoon baking soda
1	cup buttermilk

Sift together flour, baking powder, sugar and salt into medium bowl. Cut in shortening with pastry blender until mixture resembles coarse meal. Dissolve soda in buttermilk and pour evenly over flour mixture, stirring until dry ingredients are moistened. Turn dough out onto floured surface and knead 10 to 12 times. Roll out dough ½ inch thick. Cut with 2 inch biscuit cutter for dinner size or 1½ inch cutter for cocktail size. Bake in preheated 450 degree oven for 10 minutes or until lightly browned.

Can be buttered while hot and frozen for later use.

Dot Addison, Atlanta, GA

CINNAMON BUTTER

½ cup butter, softened
⅔ cup cinnamon chips
2 tablespoons whipping cream

Beat butter at medium speed with electric mixer until creamy. Microwave cinnamon chips and whipping cream in glass bowl at HIGH for 1 minute, stirring once. Stir until blended; cool. Stir together butter and cinnamon mixture; cover and chill. Serve at room temperature.

Onion Crescent Crunch Sticks

2	eggs, slightly beaten
2	tablespoons butter, melted
1	teaspoon flour
½	teaspoon garlic salt
½	teaspoon parsley flakes
¼	teaspoon onion salt
1	8-ounce can refrigerated crescent dinner rolls
2	3-ounce cans French fried onions, crushed

Combine eggs, butter, flour, garlic salt, parsley flakes and onion salt. Separate crescent dough into 4 rectangles. Firmly press perforations to seal. Cut each rectangle crosswise into 8 strips. Dip each strip into the egg mixture. Coat with crushed onions. Place on ungreased baking sheets. Bake in preheated 375 degree oven for 8 to 12 minutes until golden brown. Immediately remove from baking sheet. Serve warm.

Elaine Bennett, Atlanta, GA

Focaccia

YEAST EQUIVALENTS

*¼-ounce package active
dry yeast =1 scant
tablespoon=1.6 ounces
compressed fresh yeast*

3	cups bread flour
1	packet (or 1 tablespoon) instant yeast
1	tablespoon sugar
2	teaspoons salt
1⅓	cups water
3	tablespoons olive or vegetable oil, divided
	herbs of choice
	grated Parmesan cheese (optional)

Mix together flour, yeast, sugar, and salt. Add water and 2 tablespoons oil and mix until ingredients are combined. Place onto floured board and knead until dough becomes smooth and elastic, about 10 minutes. Form into ball and place into oiled bowl, turning once to coat both side of ball. Cover and place in warm spot, away from drafts, to rise until it doubles in bulk, about 45 minutes. Once it has risen, coat a 13x9 ½ inch baking sheet with oil. Turn dough onto sheet and pat down evenly to completely fill baking sheet. Brush with remaining oil and then, using fingertips, press lightly all over dough to make "dimples." Sprinkle with rosemary or your favorite herb and Parmesan cheese or, if you prefer, coarse salt. You may also simply add the herbs to the dry ingredients before adding the water and oil. Cover lightly and set in warm, draft-free spot to rise for 20 minutes. Once it has risen again, place in preheated 350 degree oven and bake 20 to 25 minutes or until light golden brown. If you prefer, leave it in a bit longer for a darker brown, crispier crust.

All-purpose flour may be substituted, but the taste and texture will be different. Bread flour gives the best results.

This recipe makes a good pizza dough as well. Once you've patted it to the desired thickness, add your favorite toppings, let it rise and then pop it into the oven on a vented pizza pan, pizza stone or baking sheet.

Carol Lindsey, Atlanta, GA

Frozen Yeast Rolls

1	package dry yeast
½	cup very hot water
½	cup margarine
¼	cup sugar
1½	teaspoons salt
½	cup very hot milk
1	egg, beaten
3½	cups unsifted flour

In a small bowl, sprinkle yeast over hot, but not boiling, water. Do not stir. Put margarine, sugar and salt in a large bowl. When yeast mixture has bubbled up, pour hot milk over the margarine, sugar and salt; add yeast mixture and egg. Sift in flour, beating after each cup. Dough should be stiff. Cover and let rise at room temperature for 2 hours. Knead a few minutes on floured board until dough no longer sticks to the board. Roll out and cut with round cookie cutter. Dip each round in melted butter, fold over to parker house shape and place on ungreased baking sheet. Do not let rolls touch each other. Cover and put in freezer. When frozen, place into freezer bags and return to freezer. When ready to cook, thaw on a baking sheet, let rise for 2 hours and bake in preheated 425 degree oven for 15 to 20 minutes.

Sue Freeman, Atlanta, GA

Quick Monkey Bread

¾	cup chopped pecans, divided
½	cup sugar
1	teaspoon cinnamon
3	10-ounce cans refrigerator buttermilk biscuits
1	cup brown sugar, firmly packed
½	cup butter, melted

Grease a 10 inch Bundt pan; sprinkle ½ cup chopped pecans evenly in bottom of pan. In shallow dish, combine sugar and cinnamon. Separate biscuits and cut into quarters. Roll each piece in cinnamon and sugar mixture and layer in pan, sprinkling remaining pecans through layers of dough. Combine brown sugar and butter and pour over dough in pan. Bake in preheated 350 degree oven for 30 to 40 minutes. Cool bread in pan for 10 minutes and then invert onto serving dish.

Margaret Bethea, Atlanta, GA

POPOVERS

3 eggs
1½ cups milk at room temperature
1½ cups flour
pinch of salt

Do not preheat oven. Beat eggs with wire whisk or hand mixer until lemon colored and foamy. Add milk to eggs and stir until well blended. Add flour and salt and mix again until foamy and smooth on top. Spray popover tins with cooking spray. Pour batter into greased popover tin. Place into cold oven, turn to 450 degrees and bake 15 minutes; reduce heat to 350 degrees and continue baking for 30 minutes. Do not open oven while cooking or popovers will fall.

Makes 6 to 8

Lois Puckett, Atlanta, GA

Almond Brickle Coffee Cake

The steady heat of a convection oven gives popovers extra loft. Most baked goods benefit from a convection oven, especially those, like popovers, that need a rapid rise.

Cake

1½	cups sugar
¾	cups butter, softened
4	eggs
1	teaspoon almond extract
1	teaspoon vanilla extract
3	cups flour
1½	cups sour cream
1½	teaspoons baking powder
1½	teaspoons baking soda
¼	teaspoon salt

Streusel

½	cup chopped dried apricots, divided
½	cup sliced toasted almonds, divided
½	cup almond brickle bits, divided

Glaze

½	cup powdered sugar
¼	teaspoon almond extract
2-3	teaspoons milk

To prepare cake, combine in large mixer bowl sugar, butter, eggs, almond and vanilla extracts. Beat at medium speed, scraping bowl often, until well mixed, 2 to 3 minutes. Add flour, sour cream, baking powder, baking soda and salt. Continue beating, scraping bowl often, until well mixed, 1 to 2 minutes. Spread ¼ batter into each of 2 greased and floured 9 inch round cake pans. Sprinkle ¼ cup apricots over batter in each pan. Sprinkle 2 tablespoons almonds and 2 tablespoons almond brickle bits over apricots in each pan. Spread remaining ¼ batter over streusel filling in each pan; sprinkle with remaining almonds and almond brickle bits. Bake in preheated 350 degree oven for 30 to 40 minutes or until toothpick inserted in center comes out clean. Cool 10 minutes; remove from pans. Cool completely. To prepare glaze, stir together in small bowl powdered sugar, almond extract and enough milk for glazing consistency. Drizzle over cooled coffee cakes.

Serves 16

1½ cups fresh raspberries can be substituted for ½ cup chopped dried apricots.

Blueberry and Cream Cheese Coffee Cake

Cake

1¼	cups sugar
½	cup butter
2	eggs
2¼	cups flour, divided
1	teaspoon baking powder
1	teaspoon salt
¼	cup milk
¼	cup water
2	cups blueberries
1	8-ounce package cream cheese, cubed

Topping

¼	cup sugar
¼	cup flour
2	tablespoons butter, melted
½	teaspoon cinnamon

To prepare cake, cream sugar and butter; add eggs and mix well. Combine 2 cups flour, baking powder and salt; add to sugar mixture, along with milk and water. Mix well. Toss blueberries in remaining flour. Fold blueberries and cream cheese into batter. Pour into greased 9x13 inch baking dish. To prepare topping, combine sugar, flour, butter and cinnamon. Crumble over batter. Bake in preheated 375 degree oven for 1 hour.

Deborah Sharkey, Columbia, MD

Double Cream Raspberry Coffee Cake

To soften an 8-ounce package of cream cheese, remove the wrapper and place cream cheese on a microwave safe plate. Microwave on high 15 seconds.

Cake

2¼	cups flour
¾	cup sugar
¾	cup butter, softened
1	cup sour cream
1	egg
½	teaspoon baking powder
½	teaspoon baking soda
¼	teaspoon salt
1	teaspoon almond extract

Filling

¼	cup sugar
1	8-ounce package cream cheese, softened
1	egg
½	cup raspberry preserves
½	cup sliced almonds

To prepare cake, stir together in large mixer bowl flour and sugar; cut in butter until crumbly. Reserve 1 cup mixture for topping. Add sour cream, egg, baking powder, soda, salt and almond extract to remaining crumb mixture. Beat at medium speed, scraping bowl often, until well mixed, 1 to 2 minutes. Spread batter over bottom and 2 inches up side of greased and floured 9 inch springform pan. To prepare filling, combine in small mixer bowl sugar, cream cheese and egg. Beat at medium speed, scraping bowl often, until smooth, 1 to 2 minutes. Spread cream cheese mixture over batter to within ½ inch of edge. Spread preserves over cream cheese mixture. Sprinkle almonds and reserved crumb mixture over preserves. Bake in preheated 350 degree oven for 45 to 60 minutes or until cream cheese filling is set and cake is dark golden brown. Cool 15 minutes; remove side of pan. Center will settle slightly. Serve warm or cold. Store in refrigerator.

Serves 16

Apricot Almond Sour Cream Coffee Cake

Cake
¾	cup brown sugar, firmly packed
½	cup butter, softened
¾	cup almond paste
1⅓	cups sour cream
½	cup apricot preserves
2	eggs
2¼	cups flour
1	tablespoon baking powder
½	teaspoon salt
¾	cup chopped dried apricots

Glaze
½	cup powdered sugar
¼	cup apricot preserves
¼-½	teaspoon water

To prepare cake, combine in large mixer bowl brown sugar and butter. Beat at medium speed, scraping bowl often, until creamy, 1 to 2 minutes. Add almond paste; continue beating, scraping bowl often, until well mixed, 1 to 2 minutes. Reduce speed to low. Add sour cream, preserves and eggs. Continue beating 1 minute. In medium bowl stir together flour, baking powder and salt; stir in dried apricots. Add to butter mixture. Continue beating 30 seconds. Pour into greased and floured 12 cup Bundt pan. Bake in preheated 350 degree oven for 50 to 60 minutes or until toothpick inserted in center comes out clean. Cool 10 minutes; remove from pan. Cool completely. To prepare glaze, stir together in small bowl powdered sugar, preserves and enough water for glazing consistency. Drizzle over cooled coffee cake.

Serves 16

"My goal was to return to work, and everyone at Shepherd helped me get there. This is the happiest I've been in a long time."

Amanda Coronado, former ABI patient

Amaretto French Toast

6	slices French bread 1 inch thick
4	large eggs
½	cup milk
1	tablespoon dark brown sugar
1	teaspoon almond extract
½	teaspoon ground nutmeg
2	tablespoons amaretto (optional)
3	tablespoons unsalted butter
¼	cup sliced almonds, toasted
	powdered sugar
	maple syrup, warmed

Arrange bread slices in lightly greased 9x13 inch baking dish. Whisk together eggs, milk, sugar, almond extract, nutmeg and amaretto; pour over bread. Let stand 3 minutes; then gently turn bread over in pan to evenly absorb egg mixture. Refrigerate overnight if desired. Melt butter in 400 degree oven in a 15x10 inch jelly-roll pan; add soaked bread. Bake for 15 minutes; turn. Bake 8 more minutes or until golden. Sprinkle with almonds and powdered sugar. Serve with syrup.

Serves 3

Susan Taulman, Atlanta, GA

Day-Before Blueberry French Toast

1	loaf French bread
6	eggs
3	cups milk
2	teaspoons vanilla extract
1	cup brown sugar, lightly packed
4	cups fresh or frozen blueberries, divided
1	cup chopped pecans or walnuts
2	cups maple syrup

The day or evening before serving, cut bread into 1 inch slices. Place in single layer in lightly greased 9x13 inch baking dish. Break eggs into mixing bowl and beat slightly; mix in milk and vanilla. Pour egg mixture over bread, cover and refrigerate overnight. In the morning, sprinkle brown sugar over bread, then top with 2 cups blueberries and chopped nuts. Bake in preheated 350 degree oven for 45 to 50 minutes, until bread has puffed slightly. In small saucepan, heat syrup and remaining blueberries over medium heat. Serve with French toast.

Serves 10

Suzanne Bible, Atlanta, GA

Baked French Toast Casserole with Praline Topping

French Toast

1	loaf French bread cut into 1 inch slices
8	large eggs
2	cups half & half
1	cup milk
2	tablespoons sugar
1	teaspoon vanilla extract
¼	teaspoon cinnamon
¼	teaspoon nutmeg
	dash of salt

Praline Topping

1	cup butter
1	cup brown sugar
1	cup chopped pecans
2	tablespoons light corn syrup
½	teaspoon cinnamon
½	teaspoon nutmeg

To prepare French toast, arrange bread slices into well buttered 9x13 inch baking dish, having 2 rows overlapping. In large bowl, combine eggs, half & half, milk, sugar, vanilla, cinnamon, nutmeg and salt. Beat ingredients until well blended but not bubbly. Pour over bread slices. Cover and refrigerate overnight. To prepare topping, combine butter, brown sugar, pecans, corn syrup, cinnamon and nutmeg, mixing well. Pour over bread slices and bake in preheated 350 degree oven for about 40 minutes, or until top is bubbly and lightly browned. Serve with maple syrup.

This casserole is great with mixed fruit or berries.

Ginny Ellithorp, Atlanta, GA

"If I met someone else who was just injured like me, I'd tell them that attitude and belief are key. This is not just a physical challenge, but a mental one. You have to believe that regardless of what happens, you'll be okay."

Dan Cunane,
former SCI patient

Cheese Blintz

Crêpes
2½	cups flour
8	eggs
3	cups milk
¾	cup butter
1	cup sugar
4	tablespoons vanilla extract

Cheese Filling
1	8-ounce package cream cheese
½	cup cottage cheese
1	cup sugar
½	teaspoon lemon zest
½	teaspoon orange zest

To prepare crêpes, combine and mix flour, eggs, milk, butter, sugar and vanilla; strain through mesh strainer. Heat 8 inch sauté pan. Add small amount of oil. Add ⅛ cup batter and cook until light golden brown; turn and cook. Remove from pan and set aside to cool. To prepare filling, combine cream cheese, cottage cheese, sugar, lemon zest and orange zest. Place small amount of filling at base of crêpe. Fold bottom to cover filling. Fold in sides and roll to close. Bake in preheated 350 degree oven until warm.

Joseph Geonczy, Pastry Chef, 103 West, Atlanta, GA

Soufflé of Jalapeño Grits

2½	cups water
½	teaspoon salt
½	cup regular grits
1	8-ounce hot Mexican processed cheese loaf
¼	cup butter
2	eggs, thoroughly beaten
½	teaspoon Worcestershire sauce
	dash of hot pepper sauce
	paprika

Bring water to a boil and stir in salt and grits; cover and reduce heat to medium high. Cook for 10 minutes. Remove from heat; add cheese and butter. Stir until melted. Add eggs, Worcestershire and pepper sauce. Blend and pour into greased 1½ quart baking dish. Sprinkle with paprika and bake in preheated 350 degree oven for 40 to 50 minutes or until set. Cool 10 minutes before serving.

Florence Inman, Atlanta, GA

Cinnamon Twists

Twists
¼   cup firmly packed brown sugar
2   tablespoons margarine or butter, softened
2   teaspoons cinnamon
1   8-ounce can refrigerated crescent dinner rolls

Glaze
¾   cup powdered sugar
1   tablespoon butter, melted
1-2   tablespoons hot water or lemon juice

To prepare twists, combine brown sugar, butter and cinnamon in small bowl. Separate crescent roll dough into 4 rectangles; firmly press perforation to seal. Spread 2 rectangles with butter mixture. Place remaining 2 rectangles on top; lightly press together. Cut each rectangle crosswise into 8 strips. Twist each strip tightly several times; seal ends. Place on greased baking sheet. Bake in preheated 375 degree oven for 10 to 15 minutes until golden brown. Immediately remove from baking sheet. To prepare glaze, combine powdered sugar and butter; add enough water or lemon juice to make spreading consistency. Spread over warm twists.

Makes 16

Joyce Preston, Kansas City, MO

Quick & Easy Omelet

Crack 2 eggs (Not more than 2) into zip top plastic bag and shake to combine. Add a variety of chopped ingredients such as cheese, ham, onions, green or red peppers, tomatoes, etc.; shake to mix and zip bag closed, making sure all air is removed. Place bag into rolling, boiling water for exactly 13 minutes. (You can cook 6 to 8 omelets in a large pot.) Open bag and omelet will roll out easily.

This recipe is great for a family brunch as everyone's omelet will be ready at the same time.

Let everyone fill their own bag and write their name on the bag with a permanent marker before cooking.

Sticky Buns

Danish Dough

1½	ounces yeast
1	cup whole milk, divided
½	cup unsalted butter
½	cup sugar
	pinch of salt
1	ounce nonfat dry milk powder
3	eggs
5	cups bread flour
½	cup cake flour

Filling

½	cup unsalted butter
½	cup light brown sugar
1	teaspoon orange zest
⅛	cup orange juice
¼	cup pecan pieces
½	cup apricot glaze
¼	cup dark raisins
¼	cup golden raisins

Caramel Glaze

1	cup unsalted butter
1	cup light brown sugar

Ingredients should be at room temperature to start. To prepare dough, place yeast in ½ cup milk in small bowl and set aside. In mixer, combine butter, sugar, salt and dry milk powder until well creamed. Add eggs one at a time until incorporated. Add remaining milk and mix briefly. Add flour and then yeast mixture to bowl and mix until smooth. Cover with plastic wrap and allow to rise for 1½ hours. Divide dough in half and roll out each piece into 9x12 inch rectangle about ¼ inch thick on a floured work surface. Brush away excess flour and place in freezer until stiff. To prepare filling, cream together butter, brown sugar and orange zest until light and fluffy. Slowly add orange juice until incorporated. To prepare caramel glaze, melt butter and mix with brown sugar until smooth; keep warm. Remove dough from freezer and spread creamed butter mixture, then apricot glaze evenly over both sheets. Sprinkle with raisins and pecan pieces. Roll dough starting from the long side so you have a 12 inch long log. Pour caramel glaze evenly over 9x12 inch baking pan. Cut dough roll into 1 inch thick pieces and place on top of caramel glaze in pan. Bake in 375 degree oven for 12 to 15 minutes or until golden brown on top. Remove from oven and cool. Invert the finished sticky buns and coat with any remaining glaze in pan. Serve warm.

Makes 2 dozen

This is a very famous recipe around Atlanta.

Jay Yarbrough, CEC, Piedmont Driving Club, Atlanta, GA

Artichoke Strata

2	tablespoons melted butter
½	cup dry breadcrumbs
1	medium onion, chopped
4	tablespoons butter
2	15-ounce cans artichoke hearts, not marinated, drained and quartered
9	eggs, beaten
4	cups shredded sharp Cheddar cheese
2	tablespoons fresh chopped parsley
	pinch of salt

For easier grating of Cheddar cheese, place it in the freezer for 10 to 15 minutes.

Combine melted butter and breadcrumbs; set aside. Sauté onion in butter. Combine onion with artichokes, eggs, cheese, parsley and salt. Mix gently and pour into ungreased 9x13 inch baking dish. This can be refrigerated overnight if desired. Top strata with bread crumb mixture and bake in preheated 350 degree oven for 35 to 40 minutes. Let stand 10 minutes and cut into squares.

If using a glass baking dish, cut oven temperature to 325 degrees.

Deborah Sharkey, Columbia, MD

Cheese Strata

⅓	cup butter, softened
10	slices white bread, crusts off
3	cups shredded sharp Cheddar cheese
4	eggs, slightly beaten
3	cups milk
1½	teaspoons salt
1	teaspoon dry mustard
	pinch of cayenne pepper
	chopped parsley
	paprika

Butter bread slices and cut each slice into 4 strips. In buttered 2 quart casserole dish, alternate layers of bread strips with cheese, ending with cheese. Beat eggs with milk, salt, mustard and cayenne; pour over layers of bread and cheese. Chill for 24 hours. When ready to cook, let stand at room temperature for 1 hour. Sprinkle with parsley and paprika. Bake in preheated 350 degree oven for 40 to 50 minutes or until puffed and brown.

Serves 6

Sausage and Mushroom Strata

6	eggs, beaten
2	cups milk
1	teaspoon dry mustard
	salt and pepper to taste
5	slices bread broken into pieces
1	pound sausage, browned and drained
1½	cups grated sharp Cheddar cheese
1	8-ounce package fresh sliced mushrooms
	paprika

Beat together eggs, milk, mustard, salt and pepper. Add bread and stir to soften. Stir in browned sausage, cheese and mushrooms. Pour into greased 9x13 inch glass baking dish. Sprinkle with paprika; cover and refrigerate overnight. In the morning, uncover and bake in preheated 350 degree oven for 40 to 45 minutes. Serve hot.

Serves 6 to 8

Cathy Williams, Marietta, GA

Spinach and Feta Cheese Quiche

1	cup feta cheese, well rinsed, patted dry and crumbled
½	cup Parmesan cheese plus extra for topping quiche
½	cup chopped green onion plus extra for topping quiche
½	cup minced fresh parsley plus extra for topping quiche
¼	cup fresh breadcrumbs
1	10-ounce package frozen chopped spinach, thawed and squeezed dry
1½	cups grated Monterey Jack cheese
1	9-inch deep-dish pie shell
1	cup half & half
4	eggs

Combine feta cheese, Parmesan cheese, green onion, parsley, breadcrumbs and spinach in mixing bowl and blend well. Sprinkle Monterey Jack cheese on pie shell. Spoon spinach mixture over top. Heat cream. Beat eggs and add warm cream, beating well. Slowly pour over spinach mixture, allowing spinach to absorb liquid before adding more. Sprinkle top with extra Parmesan, onion and parsley. Bake in preheated 375 degree oven for 1 hour. Let stand 5 minutes before serving.

Carol Sharkey, Atlanta, GA

MEXICAN QUICHE

½ cup butter or margarine, melted

12 eggs

2 cups small curd cottage cheese

½ cup flour

1 teaspoon salt or onion salt

1 teaspoon baking powder

1 8-ounce can diced green chilies

4 cups shredded Monterey Jack cheese

Combine butter, eggs, cottage cheese; stir in flour, salt and baking powder until well combined. Stir in green chilies and cheese. Pour into greased 9x13 inch baking dish and bake in preheated 350 degree oven for 40 to 45 minutes.

Sharon Tatom, Tuscon, AZ

Appetizers and Beverages

HOSPITALITY

Cheese Wafers

2½   cups grated extra sharp Cheddar cheese
1   cup flour
½   teaspoon salt
1   teaspoon baking powder
¼   teaspoon red pepper
½   teaspoon Worcestershire sauce
¼   teaspoon paprika
1   cup crushed cornflakes cereal
6   tablespoons margarine, softened

In large bowl, mix cheese, flour, salt, baking powder, pepper, Worcestershire, paprika, cereal and margarine together and drop by teaspoonfuls onto ungreased baking sheet. Flatten each with fork. Bake in preheated 300 degree oven for 18 to 20 minutes.

Marian Stevens, Atlanta, GA

Buffalo Chicken Dip

2   skinless, boneless chicken breasts
¾   cup hot pepper sauce
1   8-ounce package cream cheese, softened
2   cups shredded sharp Cheddar cheese, divided
1   cup Ranch or bleu cheese dressing

In large saucepan, boil chicken 8 to 10 minutes. Remove from water, cool and shred. Add chicken and pepper sauce to saucepan over medium heat. Stir in cream cheese and combine well. Add 1 cup Cheddar cheese and stir until melted. Add dressing and stir until combined. Pour into greased 11x7 inch baking dish and top with remaining Cheddar cheese. Bake in preheated 350 degree oven for 25 to 30 minutes or until bubbling.

This dip can be served with celery sticks, corn chips or shredded wheat crackers.
Julie I. Mitchell, Atlanta, GA

Quick Cheese Spread

1 8-ounce package
cream cheese

1 5-ounce jar Roka
cheese spread

1 5-ounce jar sharp,
processed cheese spread

chopped pecans

Blend cream cheese, cheese spread and processed cheese spread together in food processor. Shape into a mound on serving plate and sprinkle with pecans. Serve with assorted crackers.

Kathy Grant,
Gladstone, MO

"Plains Special" Cheese Ring
A Jimmy Carter Family Favorite

4	cups grated sharp Cheddar cheese
1	cup mayonnaise
1	cup finely chopped nuts
1	small onion, finely grated
	black pepper and cayenne pepper to taste
	strawberry preserves

In a large bowl, combine cheese, mayonnaise, nuts, onion, pepper and cayenne. Mix well, mold into ring and refrigerate until firm for several hours or overnight. Fill center with strawberry preserves and serve with crackers on the side.

Rosalynn Carter, Former First Lady, Plains, GA

Fruit and Nut Cheese Ball

2	8-ounce packages cream cheese
2	cups grated Monterey Jack cheese
½	cup chopped dried apricots
½	cup chopped dried dates
½	cup chopped raisins
⅔	cup chopped pecans

Mix cream cheese and Monterey Jack cheese in mixer until blended. Add dried apricots, dates and raisins and refrigerate 2 hours until set. Remove from refrigerator, form into ball and roll in chopped pecans. Serve with crackers.

Dried cranberries can be used in place of raisins.

Low fat cream cheese can be substituted for regular cream cheese.

Martha Jo Katz, Atlanta, GA

Bleu Cheese Dip

1	cup bleu cheese, room temperature, divided
½	8-ounce package cream cheese, room temperature
1	cup mayonnaise
¾	cup light cream or half & half

Combine ½ cup bleu cheese with cream cheese and mix thoroughly. Add mayonnaise and mix. Gradually add cream. Crumble and stir in remaining bleu cheese. Chill at least 2 hours. The chunky dip will thicken as it sets. Add small amount of cream if too thick.

This dip is best served with vegetables.

Margaret Bethea, Atlanta, GA

"This cheese ring recipe is a favorite in our community. When Jimmy and I were in the Georgia Governor's Mansion, I named it the Plains Special Cheese Ring and served it on many occasions, both in the family quarters and for public events. It was a popular dish at the White House, too. So many people asked for the recipe that we eventually had it printed on cards to handle the requests."

Rosalynn Carter

Spicy Cheese Toast

1	12-inch piece of day old baguette
¼	cup olive oil
¼	teaspoon salt
1	cup coarsely grated Parmigiano-Reggiano cheese
⅛	teaspoon cayenne pepper

Cut baguette into ¼ inch thick slices, cutting on the diagonal. Arrange baguette slices in one layer on baking sheet. Brush one side of each slice with olive oil and sprinkle with salt. Bake in middle of preheated 375 degree oven for 10 minutes. Toss cheese with cayenne and sprinkle over each slice. Bake until cheese is melted and toasts are golden and crisp, about 6 to 8 minutes. Cool completely.

Elizabeth Morgan Spiegel, Atlanta, GA

Guacamole

4	ripe avocados
1½	teaspoons lemon or lime juice
1½	teaspoons garlic powder
2	teaspoons cumin
1	onion, puréed
1	tablespoon Worcestershire sauce
	salt, pepper and hot pepper sauce to taste
1	tomato, seeded and chopped
	grape tomatoes, halved
	sour cream

Peel and mash avocados, leaving some chunks. Add juice, garlic powder, cumin, onion, Worcestershire, salt, pepper and pepper sauce. Mix well. Stir in tomato and place on serving dish. Sprinkle grape tomatoes on top for color and add dollop of sour cream.

Makes 4 cups

The guacamole needs to be tightly covered and refrigerated to avoid discoloration if making ahead. It may be used as a dip with chips or as salad on bed of lettuce.
Florence Inman, Atlanta, GA

VIDALIA ONION APPETIZER

3 cups chopped Vidalia onions
3 cups shredded Swiss cheese
2 cups mayonnaise

In casserole dish, mix onion, cheese and mayonnaise together. Bake in preheated 350 degree oven for 30 minutes. Spread hot over crackers or dipper chips.

Lynne Yancey, Atlanta, GA

Cajun Seafood Dip

2	pounds chicken breasts, diced
1½	teaspoons salt, divided
2	teaspoons ground garlic
1	teaspoon cayenne pepper, divided
1¼	cups flour
1	cup vegetable oil
1	cup diced onion
1	cup diced green pepper
1	cup diced celery
½	teaspoon garlic powder
¼	cup gumbo filé
1	teaspoon minced garlic
8	cups chicken stock, chilled
½	pound Andouille sausage
1	pound shrimp, peeled, deveined and diced
	salt and pepper to taste
1	cup shredded colby cheese
4	8-ounce packages cream cheese, whipped
1	cup panko breadcrumbs

Dry rub diced chicken with 1 teaspoon salt, ground garlic and ½ teaspoon cayenne and let set for 1 hour. Coat chicken in flour; reserve ½ cup flour and discard the remainder. Heat oil on medium heat in stockpot and carefully add chicken; brown thoroughly. Remove chicken and drain on paper towel. Drain oil, measuring out ½ cup to put back in stockpot. Add oil if not ½ cup remaining. Add onion, green pepper and celery to stockpot and sauté 3 minutes. Add reserved flour, stirring continuously, about 5 minutes, until roux starts to brown. Add one at a time remaining salt, garlic powder, remaining cayenne, gumbo filé and garlic, stirring to incorporate each into roux. Slowly add chicken stock with wire whisk, stirring constantly until smooth and thickened. Bring to boil. Add chicken, Andouille sausage and diced shrimp; reduce heat and simmer, stirring frequently, for 30 to 45minutes. Adjust salt and pepper. Cool slightly. In food processor, in batches, quickly blend all of base to keep some body. Cool completely. In mixer with paddle attachment, fold small amounts of base into small amounts of colby cheese and cream cheese until all is mixed. Pour into greased baking dish and cover with breadcrumbs. Bake in preheated 350 degree oven until top browns and dip is hot throughout.

Ron Horgan, CEC, Ansley Golf Club, Atlanta, GA

East Indian Dip

½	cup orange marmalade
3	tablespoons cider vinegar
2	tablespoons sugar
1	tablespoon brown sugar
½	teaspoon salt
¼	teaspoon curry powder
¼	teaspoon ginger
1½	teaspoons Worcestershire sauce
⅓	cup sour cream

In small saucepan, combine marmalade, vinegar, sugar, brown sugar, salt, curry powder, ginger and Worcestershire. Bring to boil and simmer, stirring constantly until marmalade melts. Let cool and mix in sour cream. Let stand. If it does not thicken enough, cream cheese may be added to correct the consistency.

This dip is good served with crackers or pita chips.

Betty Besten, Louisville, KY

Spinach Dip in Pumpernickel Boat

1	10-ounce package frozen chopped spinach
1	cup sour cream
1	tablespoon lemon juice
1	cup mayonnaise
½	cup dried chopped chives
½	tablespoon dill seed
1	tablespoon oregano
1	tablespoon salad supreme seasoning
1	loaf round rye or pumpernickel bread
	lettuce leaves

Drain spinach well, pressing between layers of paper towel to remove excess moisture. In large bowl, mix spinach with sour cream, lemon juice, mayonnaise, chives, dill seed, oregano and salad supreme seasoning. Hollow center of round loaf of rye or pumpernickel bread. Line bread with lettuce leaves, fill with spinach mixture and surround with remaining bread.

Joan Ventresca, Atlanta, GA

PINEAPPLE PARTY DIP

2 8-ounce packages cream cheese, softened

1 8-ounce can crushed pineapple, well drained

15-20 pimiento-stuffed green olives, diced

1 small onion, diced

In large bowl, mix cream cheese, pineapple, olives and onion. Form into round ball and place on serving plate. Chill. Serve with crackers.

Cover with plastic wrap before shaping into ball.

Linda Putnam, Fayetteville, GA

Hot Cheese Soufflé Dip

2	cups finely grated sharp Cheddar cheese
2	cups finely grated extra sharp Cheddar cheese
1½	cups finely grated Swiss cheese
1	large onion, finely chopped
2	teaspoons garlic salt
	cayenne pepper
3	cups mayonnaise
8-10	bacon strips, cooked crisp and crumbled
	paprika
½	cup toasted pecan pieces

In large bowl, mix sharp Cheddar, extra sharp Cheddar, Swiss cheese, onion, garlic salt, cayenne and mayonnaise and stir lightly. Add bacon to cheese mixture and put into 2 to 3 quart baking dish; sprinkle with paprika. Cover with toasted pecans and bake in preheated 325 degree oven for 20 to 25 minutes until bubbly. Serve with scoop corn chips.

Serves 25 to 40

To toast pecans, lightly drizzle with butter and salt and bake in preheated 400 degree oven for 5 minutes.

Merrie Beth Donehew, Marietta, GA

Texas Caviar

2	15-ounce cans black-eyed peas, drained and rinsed
½	cup chopped onion
1	green pepper, chopped
1	green onion, chopped
½	cup chopped jalapeño peppers
1	tablespoon minced garlic
2	large tomatoes, seeded and chopped
1	cup Italian dressing

In large bowl, mix peas, onion, green pepper, green onion, jalapeño peppers, garlic, tomatoes and Italian dressing together. Serve on plate as appetizer or as dip with crackers or chips.

Ginny Wolf, Atlanta, GA

Spinach and Artichoke Dip

1   14-ounce can artichoke hearts, drained and chopped
1   9-ounce package frozen creamed spinach, thawed
½   cup grated pepper cheese
1   cup grated Monterey Jack cheese
¾   cup grated Parmesan cheese
½   teaspoon garlic powder
¼   teaspoon hot pepper sauce
1   8-ounce jar salsa

In large bowl, mix artichoke hearts, creamed spinach, pepper cheese, Monterey Jack, Parmesan, garlic powder and pepper sauce. Spoon into 10 inch pie pan and bake in preheated 350 degree oven for 30 minutes. Remove from oven and pour salsa on top. Serve with tortilla chips.

Alice Lanier, Marietta, GA

Okra Pinwheels

1-2   teaspoons cream cheese, softened and whipped
1   ham slice, sandwich thickness
1   pickled okra, ends trimmed

Spread cream cheese on sturdy ham slice. Roll pickled okra on ham slice. Roll up in aluminum foil and chill. When ready to serve, cut each roll into ¼ inch pieces.

Even people who don't like okra like these dainty bite-size pieces. These were served at Bishop Judson Child's 50th anniversary of his ordination.

Amount for each ingredient depends on how many pinwheels are needed.

Dorothy Thrower, Tyler, TX

Spiced Nuts

1 egg white
1 teaspoon water
1 16-ounce jar
dry roasted peanuts
3 teaspoons
pumpkin pie spice
1 cup sugar

In small mixing bowl, beat egg white with water. Mix in nuts to coat. Combine pumpkin pie spice with sugar. Roll nuts in sugar mixture. Put nuts on baking sheet covered in aluminum foil and bake in preheated 300 degree oven for 20 minutes. Dump on wax paper to cool and separate.

Betty Munford, Atlanta, GA

WATER CHESTNUTS
BAKED IN CHILI SAUCE

**1 pound bacon, strips
cut in half**

**1 8-ounce can whole
water chestnuts, drained**

**½ cup mayonnaise style
salad dressing**

½ cup brown sugar, packed

¼ up chili sauce

In large skillet, cook
bacon until almost crisp.
Wrap bacon around water
chestnuts and secure
with toothpicks. Place in
baking dish. For sauce,
mix salad dressing, brown
sugar and chili sauce.
Pour over water
chestnuts and bake in
preheated 350 degree
oven for 45 minutes.

Makes 24

*This dish travels really
well and is great for
potluck dinners.*

Linda Putnam,
Fayetteville, GA

Bacon-Wrapped Water Chestnuts

3	5-ounce cans water chestnuts
¾	cup soy sauce
1¼	cups brown sugar, divided
1	pound bacon
1	cup ketchup

In small bowl, marinate water chestnuts in soy sauce for 30 minutes. Drain and roll in ¼ cup brown sugar. Cut each bacon strip into 3 pieces. Wrap bacon pieces around water chestnuts and secure with toothpicks. Place on rack in broiler pan and bake in preheated 400 degree oven until bacon is crisp, turning over when one side is done. Remove and drain on paper towel. For sauce, mix remaining brown sugar and ketchup in small saucepan and simmer until hot. Serve in bowl alongside water chestnuts.

Joyce Preston, Kansas City, MO

Cold Shrimp-Vegetable Appetizer

2	cups mayonnaise
½	cup horseradish
½	teaspoon seasoned salt-flavored enhancer
2	teaspoons dry mustard
2	teaspoons lemon juice
½	teaspoon salt
1½	pounds shrimp, peeled and cooked
2	cups small cherry tomatoes
1	6-ounce can pitted black olives
1	8-ounce can whole water chestnuts
½	pound fresh mushrooms, cut in half
½	head broccoli

Mix mayonnaise, horseradish, seasoned salt, mustard, lemon juice, salt, shrimp, tomatoes, olives, water chestnuts and mushrooms. Before serving, add raw broccoli florets. Mix and serve in bowl with toothpicks.

Lynne Yancey, Atlanta, GA

Belgian Endive Spears with Duck and Apricot Salad

1	cup Duck and Apricot Salad (below)
3	heads Belgian endive
1	cup alfalfa sprouts (or any other sprouts)

Duck for Duck and Apricot Salad

1	teaspoon peeled and finely diced ginger
1½	tablespoons brown sugar
1½	tablespoons dark corn syrup
1	tablespoon pineapple juice
2	tablespoons soy sauce
1	tablespoon sesame oil
1	tablespoon white wine
1	boneless, skinless duck breast

Duck and Apricot Salad

1	duck breast, marinated
1	tablespoon toasted and chopped walnuts
1	tablespoon slivered dried apricots
2	tablespoons slivered water chestnuts
2	tablespoons diced red bell pepper
1	tablespoon leeks, white and light green parts only, thinly sliced into ½ moons
2	teaspoons julienne red onion
2	tablespoons walnut oil
1	teaspoon red vinegar
1½	teaspoons peeled, minced ginger
2	tablespoons soy sauce
½	teaspoon minced garlic
2	tablespoons honey
	pepper to taste

To prepare duck, combine ginger, brown sugar, corn syrup, pineapple juice, soy sauce, sesame oil and wine. Marinate duck breast in mixture for 1 hour; remove duck and discard marinade. Grill or sauté duck breast until done; cool. Julienne duck breast into thin strips about 1½ inches long and thickness of a kitchen match. To prepare salad, combine marinated and cooked duck breast with walnuts, apricots, water chestnuts, bell pepper, leek, onion, walnut oil, vinegar, ginger, soy sauce, garlic, honey and pepper. Cut stem end off endive. Separate leaves, keeping them whole. Place small amount of sprouts in endive and top with the duck salad, leaving some sprouts visible.

Makes 2 dozen

This recipe is usually served on a platter as an hor d'oeuvre.

Chef Andrew Snow, Feastivities Catered Events, Berwyn, PA

Caramelized Bacon

1 pound bacon, 16-18 cut

1 cup sugar

Dip bacon slice in sugar and lay on baking sheet pan lined with parchment paper and fitted with roasting rack. Bake in preheated 350 degree oven until caramelized and brown. Remove to clean tray to cool.

May be made 24 hours in advance and held in airtight container.

Kevin Walker, CMC, Cherokee Town and Country Club, Atlanta, GA

Swedish Meatballs

Meatballs

1	pound each lean ground beef, pork, and lamb
2	cups Italian breadcrumbs
1	cup finely chopped purple onion
½	cup chopped parsley
4	eggs, beaten
	salt and pepper to taste

Sauce

3	12-ounce bottles chili sauce
3	16-ounce cans whole cranberry sauce
1	cup brown sugar, tightly packed
1	cup sugar
½	cup lemon juice

To prepare meatballs, mix together beef, pork, lamb, breadcrumbs, onion, parsley, eggs, salt and pepper and mold into small meatballs. To prepare sauce, mix chili sauce, cranberry sauce, brown sugar, sugar and lemon juice together and pour over meatballs. Bake in preheated 350 degree oven for 45 minutes or until done.

Swedish meatballs is a very festive food that can be prepared ahead of time and cooked and frozen or placed in refrigerator overnight and baked the following day.

Diana Patterson, Atlanta, GA

Oysters Supreme

1	garlic clove, split
¼	cup butter
1	teaspoon chopped onion
1	teaspoon chopped chives
1	teaspoon chopped parsley
1	teaspoon tarragon
¼	teaspoon salt
¼	teaspoon pepper
¼	cup breadcrumbs
1	pint oysters, drained but juicy

Brown garlic in butter; remove and discard garlic. Add onion, chives, parsley, tarragon, salt, pepper and breadcrumbs. Cook 5 minutes. Put an oyster in each serving shell and top with 1 tablespoon mixture. Bake in preheated 400 degree oven for 10 minutes.

"I always serve this New Year's Eve with Champagne."

Serves 4

Doris Shelton, Atlanta, GA

Caponata on Crostini

1	large eggplant, cut in ½ inch cubes
1	large onion, diced
1	green pepper, seeded and diced
6	tomatoes, chopped
½	cup chopped pimiento-stuffed green olives
4	garlic cloves, chopped
¾	cup olive oil, divided
⅓	cup red wine or cider vinegar
1	teaspoon salt
3	tablespoons sugar
1½	teaspoons dried oregano
1½	teaspoons dried basil
1	tablespoon capers
½	baguette, cut into 20 ¼ inch slices

In large stainless steel pot, combine eggplant, onion, green pepper, tomatoes, olives, garlic, ½ cup olive oil, vinegar, salt, sugar, oregano, basil and capers. Mix well. Bring to boil, then reduce heat to medium low and cook uncovered, stirring occasionally, about 1 hour and 15 minutes, or until mixture is soft and all liquid has cooked away. Set aside to cool to room temperature. Preheat oven to 400 degrees and place rack about 5 inches from top of oven. Brush bread slices with remaining olive oil and place in oven for 12 minutes or until lightly browned. Remove from oven and spread caponata on each piece of bread and serve hot or at room temperature.

Caponata can be made ahead and kept tightly covered in refrigerator for up to a week, or frozen for up to 2 months until ready to use.
Makes 20

Florence Inman, Atlanta, GA

Green Chili Pie

1½	4-ounce cans whole green chilies, split into single thickness
4	cups grated Cheddar cheese
3	eggs

Line split green chilies in greased 8 inch square baking dish and cover with grated cheese. Beat eggs and pour over cheese. Bake in preheated 350 degree oven until lightly browned, 30 to 40 minutes.

Green Chili Pie is delicious served on sesame crackers
Sallie Snow, West Grove. PA

QUESADILLA PIE

1½ 4-ounce cans chopped green chilies, drained
4 cups shredded Cheddar cheese
4 eggs
2 cups milk
1 cup biscuit baking mix
sour cream, guacamole and salsa

Sprinkle chilies and cheese in greased 10 inch pie plate. Beat eggs, milk, and biscuit baking mix together, approximately ½ minute until blended. Pour mixture over cheese/chilies mix. Bake in preheated 400 degree oven for 25 to 30 minutes. Cool 10 minutes before cutting. Serve with sour cream, guacamole and salsa.

Cheryl Foos, Parker, CO

Mushroom Rolls

½   pound fresh mushrooms, finely chopped
¼   cup butter
3   tablespoons flour
¾   teaspoon salt
1   cup light cream
1   teaspoon lemon juice
½   teaspoon onion salt
1   20-ounce loaf fresh white bread
¾   cup butter, melted

Sauté mushrooms in butter for 5 minutes; cool. Add flour and blend well. Add salt and stir in cream, cooking until thick, stirring constantly. Add lemon juice and onion salt and let cool. Remove crusts from bread and roll each slice with rolling pin until flat. Spread mixture on each slice and roll up. Place on baking sheet and freeze. Remove and cut each roll into thirds. Put in plastic bag and keep frozen until ready to use. When ready to serve, remove frozen rolls, dip each in melted butter and place on baking sheet. Bake in preheated 375 degree oven for 15 to 20 minutes or until lightly brown, turning each roll midway through baking to brown evenly. Serve warm.

Makes 2½ to 4 dozen

Bev Hynes, Overland Park, KS

Pepper Jelly Tarts

1   5-ounce jar sharp, processed cheese spread
½   cup butter
1   cup flour
2   tablespoons water
1   4-ounce jar hot pepper jelly

Cut cheese and butter into flour. Quickly stir in water and shape into ball. Refrigerate overnight. Roll dough to ¼ inch thickness and cut with biscuit cutter into 2 inch circles. Place ½ teaspoon pepper jelly in center of each circle. Fold over and crimp edges with fork. Bake in preheated 375 degree oven for 8 to 10 minutes.

Tarts may be frozen and reheated.

Makes 16 to 18

May substitute orange marmalade or bacon bits for filling. Brushing egg wash over the tops before baking will make tarts look bakery-finished and more appetizing.

Dorothy Thrower, Tyler, TX

Hot Crab Salad on English Muffins

1	7-ounce can crabmeat
1	cup mayonnaise
½	cup shredded Cheddar cheese
2	chopped green onions, including green tops
½	cup chopped celery
⅓	cup chopped green pepper
3	bacon strips, fried crisp and crumbled
½	large tomato, chopped
1	hard-boiled egg, chopped
	English muffins, split

Mix together crabmeat, mayonnaise, cheese, green onion, celery, green pepper, bacon, tomato and egg. Spoon on English muffins and broil until warm and slightly brown.

Mattie Lisenby, Atlanta, GA

Country Club Saltine Crackers

saltine crackers
ice water
melted butter
seasoning salt or garlic salt
Parmesan or Romano cheese

Preheat oven to 450 degrees. Grease baking sheet. Fill large bowl with ice water. Immerse 3 or 4 crackers at a time for 30 seconds. Remove with slotted spoon and place on baking sheet. Lightly drizzle butter over crackers. Sprinkle with seasoning salt or garlic salt and cheese. Reduce heat to 400 degrees and bake for 15 minutes. Further reduce heat to 300 degrees and bake for 25 minutes until golden brown. Store in airtight container.

These are the delicious crackers served at the Piedmont Driving Club and at Capital City Country Club. The story goes that several years ago at the Capital City Country Club several cases of saltine crackers got damp in storage. The chef hated to throw them away so he put butter and salt on them and put them in the oven. They were a big success. But when he tried to make them again and used dry saltines, it didn't work; therefore, the water dipping. Everyone still loves these crackers today!

Karen Shepherd Spiegel, Atlanta, GA

CRAB WEDGES

½ cup butter, softened
1 5-ounce jar sharp, processed cheese spread
1½ teaspoons mayonnaise
garlic salt to taste
1 7-ounce can crabmeat
6 English muffins, split

Combine butter and cheese; cream well. Add mayonnaise, garlic salt and crabmeat. Spread on muffins and cut into fourths. Wedges may be frozen at this point for future use, or if using immediately, broiled until bubbly and toasted.

Makes 48

Cecilia Waddey, Atlanta, GA

Tuna Tartare

1	ripe avocado
1	tablespoon diced red onion
1½	tablespoons lemon juice, divided
	salt and pepper to taste
1	medium tomato
1	tablespoon diced onion
1	tablespoon mayonnaise
1	tablespoon prepared horseradish
2	ounces diced Ahi tuna
½	tablespoon diced peeled cucumber
¼	cup chives, plus additional for garnish
½	cup extra virgin olive oil

In small bowl, mix avocado, red onion, ½ teaspoon lemon juice, salt and pepper into a paste and set aside. Trim away outer edges of tomato, cut into small strips and dice. Mix tomato with diced onion, mayonnaise, horseradish, salt and pepper to taste. Through a sieve, drain off excess liquid and set aside. Mix diced tuna, cucumber, remaining lemon juice, salt and pepper. Set aside. Place chives in blender and blend while slowly adding olive oil. Set aside. Place 2 inch ring mold onto small plate and place tomato mixture inside mold until ⅓ full and gently press evenly with spoon. Add avocado mixture on top of tomato until another ⅓ full. Finally, put tuna mixture on top of avocado mixture to fill mold and press down with spoon. Drizzle some of remaining liquid from tomato around mold. Also, drizzle some chive oil around mold along with some clipped chives. Remove mold and serve.

Serves 1

Blue Ridge Grill, Atlanta, GA

Summertime Iced Tea

6	cups boiling water
6	tea bags or 8 if decaffeinated
1½	cups sugar, or less to taste
1	6-ounce can frozen orange juice, thawed and undiluted
1	6-ounce can frozen lemonade, thawed and undiluted
8	cups cold water

In large pan, bring water to boil, add tea bags and let sit for 5 minutes. Remove tea bags and add sugar, orange juice, lemonade and cold water. Stir to dissolve sugar. Refrigerate and serve over ice.

Margaret Bethea, Atlanta, GA

Artillery Punch

1	pound green tea
2	gallons cold water
	juice of 36 oranges
	juice of 36 lemons
5	pounds brown sugar
2	quarts maraschino cherries
3	gallons Catawba or Rhine wine
1	gallon rum
1	gallon brandy
1	gallon bourbon or rye whisky
1	gallon gin
2-3	large ceramic or glass crocks
	Champagne or soda water

Let tea steep in cold water overnight. Strain and add orange and lemon juices. Add brown sugar, cherries, wine, rum, brandy, bourbon and gin. Cover loosely; allow to stand (ferment) for 2 to 6 weeks in a cool, dark place. Strain solids and put liquid in gallon or quart jars. Mix 1 gallon of this stock with one quart champagne or soda water.

Ideal if you need to serve a large number of people (200) and don't want to have bartenders. The Chatham Artillery was Savannah's oldest military organization and was founded in the 18th century. This punch was created for the unit at some point and reputedly was served to President James Monroe during a visit to Savannah in 1819. It has a deceptively mild taste but packs quite a punch. Start preparations 2 to 6 weeks before you plan to serve it.

Park Callahan, Savannah, GA

Southern Delight Mint Julep

2	cups granulated sugar
2	cups water (branch water is ideal)
6-8	bruised fresh mint sprigs
	Kentucky Bourbon (2 ounces per serving)
	fresh mint sprigs for garnish

Boil sugar and water in saucepan over high heat for 5 minutes to make "mint syrup." Place in covered container with mint sprigs and refrigerate overnight. Make julep by filling julep cup or glass with crushed ice then adding 1 tablespoon mint syrup and 2 ounces bourbon. Stir rapidly with spoon to frost outside of cup or glass. Garnish with fresh mint sprig.

Makes 44 mint juleps

Ann Trufant, Brevard, NC

Creamy Peppermint Punch

1 quart eggnog
1 liter chilled club soda
½ gallon peppermint ice cream, softened
hard peppermint candies, crushed

Stir together eggnog, club soda and peppermint ice cream in punch bowl or large bowl; sprinkle with peppermint candy and serve immediately.

Makes 1 gallon of punch

Punch may be made ahead without crushed peppermint candies and chilled 2 hours. Stir well and sprinkle with candies just before serving.

Susan Taulman, Atlanta, GA

To bruise fresh mint sprigs, place in cup and gently pass the back of a spoon between cup and the leaves once or twice. You want the mint to release some of the fragrant oils.

White Sangría

½   cup sugar
½   cup fresh lemon juice
1   750-milliliter bottle dry white wine
⅓   cup freshly squeezed orange juice
¼   cup triple sec
1   lemon, thinly sliced
      thinly sliced orange slices, quartered strawberries and mint for
          optional fruit
1   liter club soda
      fresh mint sprigs for garnish

In large clear glass pitcher, dissolve sugar in lemon juice. Add wine, orange juice, triple sec, lemon slices and ice cubes and stir well. Just before serving, add optional fruit for color, club soda and ice cubes. Garnish each serving with fresh mint.

Florence Inman, Atlanta, GA

Spiced Iced Tea

7   gallons cold water, divided
8   cups sugar
25-30   whole cloves
18   tea bags
2   quarts orange juice (can use frozen)
3   cups lemon juice (made from frozen concentrate)
         ice cubes

Place 4 gallons cold water, sugar and cloves in large pot. Bring to boil over high heat. Stir to dissolve sugar. Reduce heat to very low, add tea bags and simmer for about 30 minutes. Remove from heat, discard tea bags and add juices and remaining cold water. Stir well and strain solids; pour over ice cubes and serve.

Serves 125

Florence Inman, Atlanta, GA

Soups and Salads

Chilled Carrot Soup Flavored with Ginger, Lump Crabmeat and Lime Chive Whipped Cream

Soup

3	medium carrots, peeled, trimmed and cut into1 inch rounds
2½	cups fresh grapefruit juice, divided
1	teaspoon butter
1	teaspoon honey
	pinch chopped fresh ginger
½	cup heavy cream
	salt and fresh ground white pepper to taste
½	cup lump crabmeat

Mousse

½	cup crème fraîche
2	teaspoons lime juice
1	tablespoon finely chopped chives

To prepare soup, put carrots, 1¼ cups grapefruit juice, butter, honey and ginger into medium pot and bring to simmer over medium heat. Reduce heat to medium low and simmer until liquid has evaporated and carrots are very soft, about 1 hour. Add cream, increase heat to medium and simmer for 3 minutes. Purée carrot mixture and remaining grapefruit juice in blender. Pass soup through a fine sieve into medium bowl and season with salt and pepper. Cover and refrigerate until chilled. To prepare mousse, whisk crème fraîche and lime juice in medium bowl until stiff peaks form. Fold in chives. Divide soup between four chilled soup bowls and place spoonful of mousse in center of each bowl on top of soup. Sprinkle lump crabmeat around mousse.

Executive Chef Christophe Joignant, The Capital City Country Club, Brookhaven, Atlanta, GA

Borscht

2	16-ounce cans sliced beets
2	14-ounce cans consommé
1	10¾-ounce can tomato soup
	onion powder, dill, salt and pepper to taste
	sour cream
	chives or parsley

In large bowl, combine beets, consommé, soup, onion powder, dill, salt and pepper. Put in blender to mix, preferably half of mixture at a time. Chill overnight. Serve with dollop of sour cream and sprinkle chopped chives or parsley over top.

This borscht is pretty, delicious and easy to prepare.
Elizabeth Neal, Rome, GA

CRÈME FRAÎCHE

**1 cup heavy cream
2 tablespoons buttermilk or sour cream**

Mix cream and buttermilk or sour cream in glass jar with lid. Screw lid on and let stand at room temperature for 8 to 24 hours or until very thick. Stir well. Cover again and refrigerate from 4 hours to 10 days.

Chilled Chardonnay and Strawberry Soup

12	ounces strawberries, washed and hulled
¼	cup honey
1½	cups Chardonnay wine
1	teaspoon fresh lime juice
2	tablespoons heavy cream
4	sprigs mint leaves

Place strawberries, honey and wine in food processor and purée until mixture is smooth. Pour mixture into bowl and refrigerate for 3 hours. Add lime juice and heavy cream and mix well. Pour soup into individual serving bowls. Garnish with mint sprigs.

Serves 4

Rhette Greenlees, Atlanta, GA

COLD STRAWBERRY SOUP

3 cups Burgundy wine

2 pints strawberries, washed, hulled and sliced

½ cup sugar

1 16-ounce carton sour cream

sour cream and strawberries for garnish

In large saucepan, simmer wine, strawberries and sugar for 30 minutes; chill. Add sour cream. Purée in blender or processor. Chill. Pour into serving bowls and garnish each with sour cream and a strawberry.

Serves 8

Cold Zucchini Soup

6	zucchini
3	cups chicken broth
2	teaspoons curry powder
1	onion, chopped
1½	cups nonfat half & half
	salt and pepper to taste

Slice zucchini and place in large saucepan. Add broth, curry powder and onion. Cook 30 minutes or until tender. Allow to cool. Purée zucchini mixture in food processor and add half & half. Add salt and pepper. Serve chilled.

Serves 8

1% milk can be used for part of the nonfat half & half.

Sarah Clarke, Atlanta, GA

Cucumber Soup

2	medium cucumbers, seeded and diced
3	onion slices
1	10¾-ounce can cream of celery soup, 99% nonfat
1	14-ounce can chicken broth, 99% nonfat
2	tablespoons fresh lemon juice
1	8-ounce carton sour cream, nonfat
	salt and pepper to taste
	dill, chives or basil

Mix cucumbers, onion, soup, broth, lemon juice, sour cream, salt and pepper in blender. Chill and sprinkle with dill, chives or basil before serving.

This recipe is very quick and easy and a good light option.

Betty Kreimer, Atlanta, GA

Gazpacho

4-5	large ripe tomatoes, peeled, seeded and chopped
1	serrano pepper, minced
2	garlic cloves, minced
2	lemon cucumbers, peeled, seeded and diced
1	red onion, peeled and thinly sliced
2	avocados, ripe but slightly firm, peeled and diced
4	cups light chicken broth
2	tablespoons fresh lemon juice
2	tablespoons red wine vinegar, medium acid
2	tablespoons chopped fresh basil
4	tablespoons chopped fresh cilantro
	kosher salt and black pepper, milled to taste
½	cup extra virgin olive oil

Combine tomatoes, serrano pepper, garlic, cucumbers, onion and avocados in large bowl. Add broth, lemon juice and vinegar and stir briefly. Stir in basil and cilantro and season with salt and pepper. Chill soup for at least 1 hour before serving. Remove from refrigerator, stir, and let rest for 15 minutes; fold in olive oil before serving.

James and Linda Shepherd, Atlanta, GA

CHEESE WAFERS

Shredded Parmesan cheese

Mound teaspoonful or more of cheese on greased baking sheet; repeat for each wafer. Bake in preheated 350 degree oven for 10 minutes. Remove and place on paper towel to absorb fat. When cool, serve.

These wafers are incredibly easy and delicious.

Betty Kreimer, Atlanta, GA

Gazpacho-Ft. Lauderdale's Best

	salt and pepper to taste
3	tablespoons sugar
¼	cup wine vinegar
¼	cup olive oil
1	bunch scallions, diced
2	cucumbers, seeded and diced
3	stalks celery, diced
¼	cup diced radishes
½	bell pepper, diced
½	cup chopped parsley
3	cups tomato juice
1	14-ounce can chicken broth, plus 1 can water
2	14½-ounce cans diced tomatoes
	sour cream

In large bowl, mix salt, pepper, sugar, vinegar and olive oil. Add scallions, cucumbers, celery, radishes, bell pepper and parsley. Stir in tomato juice, broth, water and tomatoes. Refrigerate 24 hours. Serve in bowls with dollop of sour cream.

For variation use cilantro in place of parsley.

Cathy Compton, Atlanta, GA

Vichyssoise

3	cups water
4	chicken or beef bouillon cubes
2	tablespoons chopped parsley, dried or fresh
1½	cups instant potatoes
2	cups half & half
1	8-ounce package light cream cheese
½	cup chopped onion
	chopped chives

In large saucepan, heat water and stir in bouillon cubes and parsley. Add instant potatoes and stir; cool for 15 minutes. Add half & half, cream cheese and onion and put into blender; blend until smooth. If too thick, add bouillon. Sprinkle chives on top before serving.

Bibba Hurst, Atlanta, GA

Similar recipe submitted by Bev Ellithorp, Atlanta, GA

Butternut Squash and Curry Soup

1	tablespoon butter
1	medium butternut squash, peeled, seeded and cut into small cubes
1	green apple, cored and cut into small pieces
1	onion, chopped
½	teaspoon sugar
½	teaspoon basil
½	teaspoon thyme
1	tablespoon curry powder
3	tablespoons white wine
1	cup chicken broth
1	cup heavy cream
1	cup milk
	salt and pepper to taste

In large saucepan over moderately low heat, add butter and sauté squash, apple, onion, sugar, basil, thyme and curry powder, stirring often, for 7 to 10 minutes, until squash is fairly soft. Add wine and broth, bring to boil and simmer for about 10 minutes, until squash is very soft. Let mixture cool, then transfer to food processor or blender and purée thoroughly. Return soup to saucepan and add cream and milk. Bring to gentle boil and simmer for about 30 minutes. Season with salt and pepper.

Serves 4 to 6

Bonnie Capsuto, Atlanta, GA

Crab Chowder

1	onion, chopped
¼	teaspoon minced garlic
¼	cup chopped green pepper
⅛	teaspoon cayenne pepper
1	tablespoon butter
2	10¾-ounce cans potato soup
1½	soup cans of milk
1	8-ounce package cream cheese
6	ounces crabmeat, or more to taste
1	15¼-ounce can whole kernel corn, undrained
⅛	cup sugar

In large saucepan, sauté onion, garlic, green pepper and cayenne in butter. Blend in soup, milk and cream cheese. Add crabmeat and corn and bring to boil. Reduce heat and simmer for 10 minutes. Stir in sugar.

Serves 6 to 8

Mary Perdue, First Lady of Georgia

Corn Chowder

4	tablespoons butter
1	cup chopped carrots
1	cup chopped celery
1	cup chopped onion
3	tablespoons flour
2	cups water
2	teaspoons garlic salt
1	teaspoon celery salt
½	teaspoon paprika
¼	teaspoon seasoned pepper
1	15¼-ounce can whole kernel corn with red and green peppers
3¼	cups shredded sharp Cheddar cheese
1	12-ounce can evaporated milk
¾	pound smoked sausage, cut into ¼ inch slices
	parsley

Melt butter in large saucepan over medium high heat. Add carrots, celery and onion and sauté until soft, 5 to 10 minutes. Stir in flour; slowly add water, stirring constantly, until thick and bubbly. Stir in garlic salt, celery salt, paprika, pepper and corn. Reduce heat and cover. Simmer, stirring occasionally, for 20 minutes. Gradually stir in cheese until melted. Stir in evaporated milk. Add sausage and cook, stirring occasionally, until warmed through. Garnish each bowl with sprig of parsley before serving.

Serves 8

May use Canadian bacon in place of sausage.

Beverly Mitchell, Atlanta, GA

Dilled Leek Soup

1	pound zucchini, coarsely chopped
1	large leek, chopped
4	tablespoons bacon fat
2	tablespoons snipped fresh dill
5½	cups chicken broth
	salt and pepper to taste
1	cup cream

In large saucepan, cook zucchini and leek in bacon fat over medium heat for 10 minutes until soft, not brown. Add dill, broth, salt and pepper. Cover and simmer for 20 minutes. Remove from heat and cool slightly. In blender or processor, purée in batches. When ready to serve, reheat and add cream. Ladle into heated bowls.

Serves 4 to 6

Joyce Preston, Kansas City, MO

Cream of Artichoke Soup

2	bunches scallions, including most of the green tops, chopped
2	tablespoons butter
2	teaspoons lemon juice
2	cups chicken broth
2	9-ounce packages frozen artichoke hearts, thawed and drained
1	teaspoon salt
½	teaspoon dried oregano
2	cups half & half
	parsley or chives

Sauté scallions in butter in deep skillet or pot. Add lemon juice and broth. Add artichokes and season with salt and oregano. Purée in batches in food processor. Add half & half and return to pot to warm. Serve with finely chopped parsley or chives. Can serve hot or cold.

For a lighter soup, a cup of nonfat half & half can be used with a cup of half & half for 2 cups total.

Triff Phillips, Smyrna, GA

German Potato and Leek Soup

4	bacon strips, diced
¼	cup chopped onion
6	leeks, chopped
2	tablespoons flour
4	cups chicken broth
3	large potatoes, sliced
2	egg yolks, beaten
1	cup sour cream
1	tablespoon parsley
2	tablespoons chervil

In Dutch oven, cook bacon. Add onion and leeks and cook 5 minutes; stir in flour. Add broth slowly, stirring constantly. Add potatoes and simmer 1 hour. Combine egg yolks and sour cream; stir into soup mixture. Simmer 5 minutes; add parsley and chervil and simmer for 5 additional minutes. Serve in bowls garnished with additional parsley or chervil.

Serves 6 to 8

Shirley Heerman, Atlanta, GA

Hungarian Mushroom Soup

2	cups onions, chopped
4	tablespoons butter, divided
12	ounces mushrooms
1-2	teaspoons dill weed
2	cups beef broth, divided
1	tablespoon tamari
1	tablespoon paprika
3	tablespoons flour
1	cup milk
1	teaspoon salt
	black pepper to taste
2	teaspoons fresh lemon juice
½	cup sour cream
¼	cup chopped parsley

In large skillet, sauté onion in 2 tablespoons butter. Add mushrooms, dill, ½ cup broth, tamari and paprika. Cover and simmer 15 minutes. Melt remaining butter in large saucepan; whisk in flour and continue whisking for a few minutes. Add milk and continue cooking, stirring frequently over low heat until thick, about 10 minutes. Stir in mushroom mixture and remaining broth. Simmer 10 to 15 minutes. Just before serving add salt, pepper, lemon juice, sour cream and extra dill, if desired. Serve garnished with parsley.

Light soy sauce may be substituted for the tamari.

Sary Newman, Marietta, GA

Potage Senaglese

1	small onion, chopped
1	small apple, chopped
3	cups clear chicken broth
1	10½-ounce can green pea soup
1	cup milk
	butter
2	teaspoons curry powder
	salt and pepper to taste

Put onion and apple in blender with broth and undiluted soup. Add milk. Beat until thoroughly blended. Add small piece of butter, curry powder, salt and pepper. Heat.

Serves 4 to 6

Nancy Montgomery, Atlanta, GA

Potage de Pois au Champagne

12	cups water
8	beef boullion cubes
2	16-ounce bags frozen green peas
2	cups Champagne, fairly dry
2	cups crème fraîche or whipping cream
	salt and pepper to taste
	parsley, finely chopped

Put water, boullion cubes and peas in large pot over medium high heat. Bring to boil. This takes about 45 minutes. Remove from heat and purée in food processor. Drain through very fine sieve into large pot. Press hard with wooden spoon to get all juice. Throw away pulp. When ready to serve, pour warmed Champagne into hot strained pea liquid. Ladle into warmed, shallow soup plates. Add slightly warmed crème fraîche to each bowl and season with salt and pepper. Sprinkle parsley on each for color.

This recipe was given to Patrick by the Palace chef and was served at the wedding feast of King Baudouin and Fabiola in the early 60's. It is easy and elegant.

Patrick T. VanBiesen, Brussels, Belgium and Atlanta, GA

Pumpkin Soup

1	tablespoon butter
1	onion, finely chopped
2	garlic cloves, crushed
1	tablespoon curry powder
1	teaspoon ginger
1	teaspoon nutmeg
1	teaspoon cumin
1	25-ounce jar unsweetened applesauce
3	15-ounce cans pumpkin
3½	cups chicken broth
1	tablespoon sugar
1	8-ounce carton yogurt

Melt butter in saucepan over medium heat and add onion, garlic, curry, ginger, nutmeg and cumin. Stir often until onion is transparent and soft. Add applesauce, pumpkin, broth and sugar. Bring to boil, stirring constantly. Cover and reduce heat to low. Simmer 20 minutes, stirring often. Remove soup and purée in blender or food processor. Return to low heat and add yogurt to warm.

Sam Harrison, Atlanta, GA

Tomato Basil Soup

4	cups canned whole tomatoes, crushed and undrained
12	fresh basil leaves
1	cup heavy cream
½	cup unsalted butter
	salt to taste
¼	teaspoon cracked black pepper

Simmer tomatoes in saucepan for 30 minutes. Purée along with basil leaves in small batches in food processor or blender. Return to saucepan and add cream and butter while stirring over low heat. Add salt and pepper. Garnish with additional basil leaves and serve with your favorite bread.

Serves 8

This recipe is easy, quick and delicious.

Hallie Pottinger Henrickson, Tin Roof Café, Villa Rica, GA

Tomato Curry Soup

2	14½-ounce cans Italian style tomatoes
1	onion, chopped
4	sprigs parsley or cilantro
6	peppercorns
1	stalk celery, chopped
2	tablespoons butter
3	tablespoons flour
2	cups evaporated milk
1	cup chicken broth
2	teaspoons curry powder
½	cup half & half

In saucepan, simmer tomatoes, onion, parsley or cilantro, peppercorns and celery for 30 minutes. While this cooks, make cream sauce by melting butter in saucepan and whisking in flour and then milk. Cook until sauce is smooth and thick. Add broth, curry powder and half & half. Process tomato mixture in blender or food processor and add to cream sauce. Reheat and serve.

Serves 8

This recipe is easy and delicious.

Kate Stradtman, Atlanta, GA

Tortilla Soup

1½	pounds boneless, skinless chicken breasts, chopped
1	large onion, chopped
2	jalapeño peppers, seeded and chopped
1	garlic clove, minced
2	large carrots, chopped
4	teaspoons vegetable oil
1	teaspoon ground cumin
1	teaspoon chili powder
1	teaspoon lemon pepper
1	teaspoon salt
1	tablespoon hot pepper sauce
½	cup flour
1	14-ounce can whole tomatoes
4	14-ounce cans chicken broth
8	corn tortillas, cut into thin strips
	oil for frying
½	cup sour cream
1	avocado, chopped
1	cup shredded Cheddar cheese
	fresh cilantro, chopped

In large saucepan, sauté chicken pieces, onion, jalapeño pepper, garlic and carrots in oil for 5 minutes. Stir in cumin, chili powder, lemon pepper, salt, pepper sauce and flour until mixed. Add tomatoes and broth and mix well. Simmer for 1 hour, stirring frequently. Fry tortilla strips in ¼ inch oil in skillet until crisp; drain. Arrange several tortilla strips in each serving bowl. Stir 1 tablespoon each of sour cream and avocado over tortilla strips. Ladle soup over layers and sprinkle with cheese and cilantro.

To decrease the caloric value of the tortilla strips, spray them with nonstick cooking spray and arrange on a baking sheet. Bake in preheated 250 degree oven until brown.

Tostado chips can be used in the place of the fried tortilla strips.

Frances Dannals Sasser, Atlanta, GA

HOSPITALITY

Vidalia Onion and Artichoke Soup

8   large Vidalia onions, peeled and sliced
2   cups butter, divided
½   cup sweet sherry
6   cups chicken broth
4   tablespoons nutmeg
1   tablespoon thyme leaves
1   tablespoon granulated garlic
4   cups heavy cream
½   cup olive oil
2   cups flour
4   14-ounce cans artichoke hearts, drained
     salt and white pepper to taste

Place onion in large pot with 1 cup butter and sauté for 20 minutes. Add sherry and cook for 5 minutes. Add broth and cook for 10 minutes. Add nutmeg, thyme, garlic and cream and bring to slow boil. In separate pot, add remaining butter and olive oil. When butter melts, add flour and stir to make roux. Cook for 5 minutes, stirring so it does not burn. Add roux to boiling soup and let thicken. Season with salt and pepper. Add artichoke hearts and heat for 10 to 15 minutes.

This recipe makes a large amount and is good for a crowd.

Chef Marty Rosenfield, Lakeside Restaurant, Highlands, NC

Nantucket Blue Salad

Dressing
1   shallot, finely chopped
1   cup blueberries
3   tablespoons sugar
⅓   cup raspberry vinegar
1   cup vegetable oil

Salad
1   10-ounce bag spinach, washed and patted dry
2   cups blueberries
½   cup crumbled bleu cheese
½   cup toasted pecan pieces

To prepare dressing, process shallot, blueberries, sugar and vinegar in blender or food processor until smooth; whisk together with oil. To prepare salad, place spinach, blueberries, cheese and pecans in large bowl. Toss with ½ the dressing and serve immediately.

Nancy Jungman, Atlanta, GA

> *"There are a lot of fun opportunities and activities at Shepherd Center, and in spite of this new challenge, you can still have a full life."*
>
> Gina Inhelder,
> former SCI patient

Spinach and Mandarin Orange Salad

Dressing
½	cup olive oil
¼	cup balsamic vinegar
¼	cup orange juice
2	teaspoons orange zest
2	tablespoons honey
3	tablespoons minced green onion
8	raspberries

Salad
1	10-ounce bag fresh baby spinach
1	8¼-ounce can Mandarin oranges, drained
¼	cup chopped nuts

To prepare dressing, combine oil, vinegar, juice, zest, honey, onion and raspberries in a jar; cover and shake to emulsify. To prepare salad, combine spinach, Mandarin oranges and nuts in a large bowl and toss with dressing.

This dressing is wonderful on any green salad.

Dianne Isakson, Marietta, GA

Spinach Salad

Dressing
¾	cup salad oil
1	tablespoon Worcestershire sauce
¼	cup sugar
⅓	cup white vinegar
⅓	cup ketchup
2	teaspoons salt
1	cup dehydrated onion

Salad
1	8-ounce can bean sprouts, drained
1	cup water chestnuts, drained and diced
2	hard-boiled eggs, chopped
¼	pound crisp bacon, crumbled
1	pound spinach, washed and chilled

To prepare dressing, combine oil, Worcestershire, sugar, vinegar, ketchup, salt and onion and chill for 12 hours. To prepare salad, combine sprouts, water chestnuts, eggs and bacon and chill; when chilled, combine with spinach in large bowl and toss with dressing.

Linda Morris, Atlanta, GA

Sunset Salad

1	bag mixed greens, romaine or baby spinach
3-4	slices purple onion
2	tablespoons sliced almonds, toasted
2	tablespoons crumbled bleu cheese
½	Fuji or other crisp apple, chopped
½	cup golden raisins
¼	red bell pepper, chopped
1	bottle Vidalia onion salad dressing

In large bowl, mix together greens, onion, almonds, cheese, apple, raisins and bell pepper; toss with dressing and serve.

Serves 4 to 6

Also good using strawberries instead of apple and bell peppers.

Martha Lou Riddle, Rome, GA

Emperor Tuna Salad

1	12-ounce can white tuna in water
1	14-ounce can artichoke hearts
1	4¼-ounce can chopped ripe olives
1	teaspoon lemon juice
1	tablespoon garlic juice
1	tablespoon onion juice
3	tablespoons olive oil
1	tablespoon mayonnaise salt and pepper to taste

Drain tuna and artichokes. Cut artichokes into small pieces. Mix tuna, artichoke hearts and olives well. Add lemon, garlic and onion juices. Mix in olive oil, mayonnaise, salt and pepper.

Excellent on toasted multi-grain bread.

Will keep in refrigerator for 3 to 5 days.

Mary Alice Alexander, Atlanta, GA

Layered Vegetable Shrimp Salad

5	cups torn lettuce
¼	cup chopped onion
½	cup mayonnaise
¼	cup sour cream
1	tablespoon sugar
¼	cup chopped celery
¼	cup chopped green bell pepper
½	cup frozen peas, thawed and drained
½	pound cooked medium shrimp
¾	cup shredded Cheddar cheese
2	bacon strips, crisply cooked and crumbled

In 8x8 inch (1½ quarts) baking dish or medium bowl, layer lettuce and onion. In small bowl, combine mayonnaise, sour cream and sugar; blend well. Spoon half of mixture evenly over lettuce and onion. Layer celery, bell pepper, peas and shrimp over mayonnaise mixture. Spread remaining mayonnaise mixture over top; sprinkle with cheese and bacon. Cover and refrigerate at least 8 hours.

Serves 6

Can substitute an 8-ounce package imitation crabmeat for shrimp.
Dolores T. Greene, Greenwich, CT

Southwestern Cornbread Salad

1	6-ounce package Mexican cornbread mix
1	1-ounce envelope buttermilk Ranch salad dressing mix
1	small head romaine lettuce, shredded
2	large tomatoes, chopped
1	15-ounce can black beans, rinsed and drained
1	15-ounce can whole kernel corn with red and green peppers, drained
1	8-ounce package shredded Mexican four cheese blend
8	bacon strips, cooked and crumbled
6	green onions, chopped

Prepare cornbread according to package directions; cool, crumble and set aside. Prepare salad dressing according to package directions. Layer a large bowl with half each of cornbread, lettuce, tomato, beans, corn, cheese, bacon and onion. Spoon half of dressing evenly over top. Repeat layers with remaining ingredients and dressing. Cover and chill at least 2 hours.

Neville S. Pearson, Atlanta, GA

Thai Meat Salad

1	pound very lean ground beef or ground turkey breast
½	cup water
½	teaspoon crushed hot pepper flakes, or more to taste
½	cup fresh chopped basil
½	cup chopped cilantro
½	cup chopped mint
1	teaspoon lime zest
2-3	tablespoons fresh lime juice
1	tablespoon fish sauce (optional)
	salt to taste
	lettuce or cabbage leaves

Crumble meat into skillet. Add water and hot pepper flakes; simmer until meat is done, mashing out lumps. Remove from heat. Cool to room temperature. Add basil, cilantro, mint, lime zest, lime juice, fish sauce and salt. Chill and serve with lettuce or cabbage leaves. To eat, roll up a small amount of salad in leaf.

Marianne Beasley

Asparagus Salad

2	envelopes unflavored gelatin
½	cup cold water
¾	cup sugar
1	10½-ounce can green asparagus tips, sliced
	liquid from canned asparagus plus enough water to measure 1 cup
½	cup white vinegar
½	teaspoon salt
1	cup chopped celery
½	cup finely chopped nuts
	juice of ½ lemon
2	teaspoons grated onion
1	2-ounce jar chopped pimiento

Dissolve gelatin in cold water. Combine sugar, asparagus liquid and vinegar in saucepan; bring to a boil. Add gelatin mixture. When cool, add salt, celery, nuts, asparagus tips, lemon juice, onion and pimiento. Pour into mold and refrigerate. Stir as gelatin thickens.

Louise M. Hicks, Atlanta, GA

Frozen Fruit Salad

3	tablespoons flour
3	tablespoons sugar
1	15-ounce can fruit salad, reserving syrup
½	cup mayonnaise
1	cup whipping cream
1	teaspoon salt
	dash of cayenne pepper
	lettuce

Blend flour and sugar. Boil syrup from fruit salad and pour over sugar and flour; beat with egg beater and put over heat until flour has thickened slightly. Add mayonnaise, whipping cream, salt and cayenne. Pour over fruit and combine; pour into ice tray or 1 quart square baking dish and freeze. Cut into squares and serve on beds of lettuce.

Serves 4 to 6

Nancy Montgomery, Atlanta, GA

"I've learned some things from all this. I know it doesn't matter how much money you make, it's your family, health and belief in God that are important."

Jeff Manka,
former SCI patient

Frozen Ice Cream Salad

1	3-ounce box lemon flavored gelatin mix
1	cup boiling water
1	pint vanilla ice cream
1	6-ounce bottle maraschino cherries, drained and chopped
1	8-ounce can crushed pineapple, drained
½	cup chopped nuts

Dissolve gelatin mix in boiling water and stir until dissolved. Add ice cream while the water is still hot. Add cherries, pineapple and nuts and mix until ice cream is melted. Pour into 5x6 inch glass dish or any 5 cup mold. Chill overnight in refrigerator until firm.

Makes a beautiful salad for holidays or special occasions.

Beth St. Jean, Marietta, GA

Mandarin Salad

1	tablespoon unflavored gelatin
½	cup water
1	11-ounce can Mandarin orange, reserving juice
1	3-ounce package lemon flavored gelatin mix
1	6-ounce can concentrated frozen orange juice
1	8-ounce can crushed pineapple
½	cup chopped pecans

Dissolve unflavored gelatin in saucepan with ½ cup water. Drain Mandarin oranges, reserving juice. Add enough water to juice to measure 1 cup; add to gelatin in saucepan. Bring to a boil and pour over lemon gelatin. Stir until well dissolved. Add orange juice concentrate and refrigerate until thickened; add oranges, pineapple and pecans. Pour into mold and refrigerate until set.

Mary Massey, Atlanta, GA

Tomato Aspic

5	envelopes unflavored gelatin
5¼	cups tomato-vegetable juice cocktail, divided
3	tablespoons lemon juice
1½	teaspoons sugar
2	bay leaves
1	slice onion, or more to taste
5	peppercorns
¾	teaspoon salt
3	tablespoons Worcestershire sauce
1	cup chopped olives
1	cup chopped celery

Dissolve gelatin in 1 cup tomato juice. Heat remaining tomato juice, lemon juice, sugar, bay leaves, onion, peppercorns, salt and Worcestershire. Simmer 5 minutes; pour in melted gelatin and strain into mold. Add olives and celery; stir to mix and refrigerate. When serving, put lettuce or other greens on large plate. Run knife around edge of aspic mold and turn upside down on greens.

Linda Lou Sumlin, Atlanta, GA

Couscous Salad

1	cup instant couscous
1	cup water
2	tablespoons fresh lemon juice
1	tablespoon champagne vinegar
3	tablespoons olive oil
¾	teaspoon salt
	pinch of pepper
1	teaspoon minced lemon zest
3	tablespoons pine nuts, toasted
1	scallion, thinly sliced
1	cup ripe cherry tomatoes, cut in half
2	tablespoons chopped flat leafed parsley or cilantro
2	tablespoons chopped fresh mint

Pour couscous into a small baking dish. Combine water, lemon juice, vinegar, olive oil, salt and pepper into small saucepan. Bring to a boil; pour over couscous and stir. Cover and set aside for 20 minutes. When couscous is ready, gently fluff with a fork to separate grains. Transfer to serving bowl and toss with lemon zest, pine nuts, scallion, tomatoes, parsley and mint.

Sarah Goodman, Atlanta, GA

German Potato Salad

2	pounds potatoes
½	cup hot beef broth
2	medium onions, diced
2	tablespoons chopped parsley
2	tablespoons chopped chives
3	tablespoons olive oil
4	tablespoons white wine vinegar
½	teaspoon salt
½	teaspoon pepper
½	teaspoon sugar
1	teaspoon mustard

Boil potatoes until fork tender, approximately 10 minutes. Do not overcook. Drain, peel and slice. Place potatoes in large bowl; pour hot broth over potatoes. Add onion, parsley and chives and stir to mix. In a small bowl, combine oil, vinegar, salt, pepper, sugar and mustard; pour over potatoes, stir gently to combine and refrigerate until cool.

Jutta Putter, Germany and Atlanta, GA

Greek Pasta Salad

Dressing
⅔   cup olive oil
3   tablespoons garlic peppercorn vinegar or white vinegar
¼   cup chopped fresh basil or 2 teaspoons dried basil leaves
2   tablespoons chopped green onions
2   tablespoons grated Parmesan cheese
½   teaspoon salt
¼   teaspoon pepper
¼   teaspoon dried oregano leaves

Salad
3   cups uncooked tri-colored spiral macaroni
1   small green bell pepper, cut into 1/4 inch strips
1   small red bell pepper, cut into 1/4 inch strips
1   medium tomato, cut into thin wedges
½   cup pitted and sliced Greek olives
1½   cups crumbled feta cheese

To prepare dressing, combine in blender or food processor olive oil, vinegar, basil, green onion, cheese, salt, pepper and oregano. Cover and blend or process until smooth; set aside. To prepare salad, cook macaroni to desired doneness as directed on package. Drain; rinse with cold water and drain. In large bowl, combine green and red peppers, tomato, olives and feta cheese. Pour dressing over salad and toss gently. Refrigerate at least 1 hour to blend flavors.

Serves 4 to 6

Jean T. Gregory, Atlanta, GA

Mediterranean Pasta Salad

Dressing
½ cup olive oil
½ cup Parmesan cheese
¼ cup Champagne or white wine vinegar
1 teaspoon minced dried oregano
2 garlic cloves, minced
1 teaspoon Dijon mustard
pepper to taste

Pasta
1 1-pound box rotini or farfalle
½ 9-ounce bag fresh spinach, torn into small pieces
2 cups crumbled feta cheese
1 bunch green onions, chopped
2 cucumbers, chopped
12 cherry tomatoes, halved
½ cup Greek olives

To prepare dressing, combine in jar oil, Parmesan cheese, vinegar, oregano, garlic, mustard and pepper and shake well. To prepare salad, cook pasta according to package directions; drain. Pour half of dressing over hot pasta and let cool. Combine spinach, feta cheese, green onion, cucumbers, tomatoes and olives in large bowl. Pour remaining salad dressing over mixture and toss with pasta. Chill. Serve chilled, at room temperature or slightly warm.

Serves 6

Jackie Fryer, Atlanta, GA

The only time pasta should be rinsed is when it is to be used in a cold pasta salad, but do drain the pasta after cooking. Leftover cooked pasta will store well if put in a plastic bag with a little oil to keep strands from sticking together.

Pasta, Chicken and Broccoli Pesto Toss

2	cups uncooked vegetable spiral pasta
2	cups cubed, cooked chicken breast
2	cups small broccoli florets, cooked tender-crisp, cooled
1½	cups shredded mozzarella cheese
⅔	cup lightly packed fresh basil leaves
2	garlic cloves
1	cup mayonnaise
1	tablespoon lemon juice
½	teaspoon salt
½	cup shredded Parmesan cheese
½	cup pine nuts or coarsely chopped walnuts, toasted

Cook pasta according to package directions until tender; drain and cool. Combine pasta, chicken, broccoli and mozzarella cheese in large bowl. Process basil and garlic in food processor until finely chopped. Add mayonnaise, lemon juice and salt. Process to combine thoroughly. Stir in Parmesan cheese; add to pasta mixture and toss to coat well. Stir in pine nuts. Serve immediately or cover and refrigerate. For maximum flavor, remove from refrigerator and toss gently 30 minutes before serving.

Serves 8
Dolores T. Greene, Greenwich, CT

Shrimp and Angel Hair Pasta

2½	cups cooked, peeled shrimp
5	cups cooked angel hair pasta
1	16-ounce can chopped black olives
4	tablespoons chopped parsley
1	cup chopped celery
2	tablespoons fresh chopped dill
	juice of ½ lime
⅓	cup red wine vinegar
1	tablespoon crushed garlic
⅓	cup olive oil
3	tablespoons Dijon mustard
4	tablespoons mayonnaise
3	tablespoons grated onion
	salt and pepper to taste

If shrimp are large, cut into small bite sized pieces. Mix together shrimp, pasta, olives, parsley, celery, dill, lime juice, vinegar, garlic, olive oil, mustard, mayonnaise, onion, salt and pepper. Refrigerate for 4 to 5 hours and serve cold.

Charles T. Pottinger, III, Atlanta, GA

Sweet Potato Salad

Salad
4	large sweet potatoes or yams, about 2 pounds
½	cup thinly sliced carrots
¼	cup sliced green onions
1	tablespoon finely chopped fresh chives
½	red bell pepper, chopped
½	green bell pepper, chopped

Dressing
½	cup oil
¼	cup mayonnaise or salad dressing
¼	cup cider vinegar
1	tablespoon lime juice
1	tablespoon coarse ground or regular prepared mustard
¼	teaspoon salt
⅛	teaspoon pepper
1	garlic clove, minced

To prepare salad, place unpeeled sweet potatoes in large saucepan; add water to cover. Bring to a boil. Reduce heat; cover and simmer 20 to 30 minutes just until potatoes are tender. Do not overcook. Drain and refrigerate 2 hours or until chilled. Peel; cut into cubes. In large bowl, combine potatoes, carrots, green onion, chives, and red and green peppers. To prepare dressing, combine oil, mayonnaise, vinegar, lime juice, mustard, salt, pepper and garlic in small jar with tight-fitting lid; shake well. Pour dressing over salad; toss to coat. Cover; refrigerate 2 hours to blend flavors. Store in refrigerator.

Sweet and Sour Potato Salad

12-15	medium red potatoes
1	16-ounce package bacon
1	large onion, thinly sliced and then quartered
1	cup vinegar
1¼	cups sugar
1	tablespoon salt
1	teaspoon pepper

Boil potatoes in water until almost done; drain and let stand covered. When potatoes are cool enough to handle, peel and slice. Slice bacon into small pieces and fry until crisp; add onion and fry until tender. Add vinegar, sugar, salt and pepper to the bacon and onion mixture and let simmer 2 to 3 minutes. Pour over potatoes; stir to mix well. Serve warm or at room temperature.

Serves 6 to 8

Joyce Crichton, Kansas City, MO

Wild Rice Salad

1½	cups uncooked wild rice
¼	cup thinly sliced green onions
¼	cup diced celery
½	cup slivered almonds, pecans or pine nuts
3	tablespoons olive oil
3	tablespoons vegetable oil
3	tablespoons white wine vinegar
¼	teaspoon dried thyme, crushed
½	teaspoon salt
¼	teaspoon pepper

Cook rice following package instructions; cool. In large bowl, combine green onion, celery and nuts with rice. In small bowl, whisk olive and vegetable oils into vinegar, one drop at a time. Stir in thyme, salt and pepper. Pour over rice mixture. Toss lightly. Serve at room temperature or chilled.

Triff Phillips, Smyrna, GA

Blueberry and Smoked Turkey Salad

Sherry Mayonnaise
1	cup mayonnaise
3	tablespoons sherry
2	teaspoons tarragon vinegar
1	teaspoon Dijon mustard
	salt and pepper to taste

Salad
1	pound smoked turkey breast
¾	pound Jarlsberg or Swiss cheese
4	stalks celery, chopped
½	cup chopped green onions
	salt and pepper to taste
4½	cups fresh blueberries

To prepare mayonnaise, combine mayonnaise, sherry, vinegar, mustard, salt and pepper. To prepare salad, cut turkey and cheese into 2 inch julienne strips; combine with celery, onion, salt and pepper. Toss with sherry mayonnaise; add blueberries and toss gently. Serve on bed of lettuce.

Mary Kay Howard, Marietta, GA

Grilled Chicken Salad with Provençal Vinaigrette

Dressing
¼   cup balsamic vinegar
½   teaspoon red pepper flakes
1   plum tomato, cored and diced
2   tablespoons minced red onion
1   garlic clove, minced
1   tablespoon drained capers
3   basil leaves, cut into very thin strips
½   cup canola oil
¼   cup olive oil
    salt and pepper to taste

Salad
6   boneless, skinless chicken breasts
1   red onion, cut into ½ inch rounds
5   tablespoons olive oil
3   tablespoons balsamic vinegar
½   cup julienne sun-dried tomatoes
1   cup drained artichoke hearts, quartered
2   tablespoons drained capers
3   plum tomatoes, cored and quartered
    salt and pepper to taste
6   large basil leaves, cut into thin strips

To prepare dressing, combine balsamic vinegar, red pepper flakes, tomato, onion, garlic, capers and basil leaves. Slowly add canola and olive oils; whisk until all oil is incorporated. Season with salt and pepper. Refrigerate until ready to use or up to 6 days. To prepare salad, toss uncooked chicken and onion with olive oil and vinegar in large bowl. Grill chicken on hot, oiled grill until juices run clear; set aside to cool. Grill onion 4 minutes per side, until slightly cooked but still crisp-tender; chop into small pieces and place in bowl. Slice chicken on the diagonal into ½ inch slices, 8 to 10 slices per breast. Add the chicken, sun-dried tomatoes, artichoke hearts, capers and tomatoes. Toss with 1 cup vinaigrette. Season with salt and pepper and garnish with basil leaves.

Deborah Ashendorf, Alpharetta, GA

Cucumber Salad

Slender, very green cucumbers will have fewer seeds, thinner skins and better taste than yellow skinned, fat ones.

3	cucumbers, peeled and seeded
2	tablespoons white vinegar
1	16-ounce carton sour cream
2	teaspoons sugar
½	teaspoon salt
1	cup chopped scallions
2	tablespoons fresh chopped dill

Slice cucumbers finely. Slowly add vinegar to sour cream until well blended. Add sugar, salt, scallions and dill. Combine cucumbers and sour cream mixture. Cover tightly and refrigerate, preferably overnight.

Robert O. Breitling, Jr., Atlanta, GA

Cucumber-Yogurt Salad

1	small garlic clove
1	teaspoon salt
1	tablespoon dried mint or 3 to 4 fresh stems and leaves
2	16-ounce cartons plain yogurt
2	cucumbers

Mash garlic with salt and fresh mint, if using. Add yogurt and blend well. Peel and cut cucumbers in half lengthwise, then slice into thin half rounds. Add cucumbers and dry mint, if using, to yogurt mixture. Fold together gently.

Serves 4

Denise Cohen, Atlanta, GA

White Meat Chicken Salad

1	cup mayonnaise
2-3	dashes of white wine vinegar
3	cups large diced warm cooked white meat chicken
½	cup chopped celery
½	cup heavy cream
	salt and white pepper to taste
	toasted almonds for garnish

Mix mayonnaise and vinegar together; combine with chicken and celery. Add cream, salt and pepper. Refrigerate. Garnish with almonds when ready to serve.

Merrie Beth Donehew, Atlanta, GA

Cauliflower Broccoli Salad

Dressing
½   cup mayonnaise
2   tablespoons sugar
1   tablespoon cider vinegar

Salad
2   cups cauliflower florets
2   cups fresh broccoli florets
½   cup raisins
¼   cup sliced green onions
¼   cup sunflower seeds
3   bacon strips, crisply cooked and crumbled

To prepare dressing, whisk together mayonnaise, sugar and vinegar. To prepare salad, combine cauliflower, broccoli, raisins, green onion, sunflower seeds and bacon and toss lightly. Pour dressing over salad mixture; toss gently to coat. Sprinkle with additional sunflower seeds, if desired. Refrigerate to let flavors blend.

Dolores T. Greene, Greenwich, CT

Edamame and Bean Salad with Shrimp and Fresh Salsa

1   cup frozen shelled edamame (soy beans)
2   cups chopped cooked shrimp
1   19-ounce can cannelloni beans, rinsed and drained
2   cups halved sweet grape tomatoes
4   tablespoons finely chopped red onion
½   jalapeño pepper, finely minced, or more to taste
4   tablespoons chopped fresh cilantro
3   tablespoons fresh lime juice
2   tablespoons extra virgin olive oil
½   teaspoon salt

Cook edamame according to package directions. Drain, rinse with cold water; drain. Combine edamame, shrimp, beans, tomatoes, onion, jalapeño pepper and cilantro. Whisk together lime juice, olive oil and salt; drizzle over edamame mixture and toss gently to coat. Cover and chill.

Serves 4

Debbie Goot, Atlanta, GA

Fresh Corn Salad

1	teaspoon salt
5	ears fresh corn (do not substitute frozen)
½	cup diced red onion
3	tablespoons cider vinegar
3	tablespoons extra virgin olive oil
½	teaspoon kosher salt
½	teaspoon freshly ground pepper
½	cup chiffonade
	fresh basil leaves (do not substitute dried)

In large pot of boiling, salted water, cook the corn for 3 minutes until starchiness is gone. Drain and immerse in ice water to stop the cooking and set color. When corn is cool, cut kernels off cob, cutting close to the cob. In a large bowl, toss corn kernels with onion, vinegar, olive oil, salt and pepper. Refrigerate. Before serving, toss in fresh basil. Taste for seasoning and serve cold or at room temperature.

Mary Ann Sikes, Atlanta, GA

Not Your Ordinary Cole Slaw

Dressing

2	garlic cloves, peeled
½	cup white vinegar
⅔	cup sugar
½	teaspoon salt
¼	teaspoon black pepper
½	cup vegetable oil

Cole Slaw

½	head green cabbage
½	cucumber, unpeeled, thinly sliced
½	large bell pepper, thinly sliced
¾	cup chopped parsley
1	cup diced celery
½	cup chopped green onions

To prepare dressing, put garlic in food processor and chop fine. Add vinegar, sugar, salt and pepper and pulse. Add oil in slow stream while processor is running. Blend until oil is well combined. To prepare cole slaw, remove outer leaves from cabbage and discard. Shred cabbage. In large bowl, mix together cabbage, cucumber, bell pepper, parsley, celery and green onion. Pour dressing over vegetable mixture and toss. Cover and refrigerate at least 4 hours or overnight. Stir slaw well and serve chilled.

Serves 8

Summer Corn and Cherry Tomato Salad

1	teaspoon salt
2	ears fresh corn
¼	cup extra virgin olive oil
1	tablespoon red wine vinegar
¼	teaspoon sugar
	salt and pepper to taste
2	cups sweet grape tomatoes, halved
2	cups cubed fresh Buffalo mozzarella cheese
2	tablespoons fresh basil, chopped

Bring large pot of water to boil. Add salt and corn. Cook for 5 minutes, then transfer to bowl of ice water. When corn is cool, drain on paper towels and set aside. Meanwhile, in a large bowl, whisk together olive oil, vinegar, sugar, salt and pepper. Add tomatoes and cheese and stir until well combined. Add corn kernels and basil and toss gently to combine.

Serves 4

Debbie Goot, Atlanta, GA

MAPLE SALAD DRESSING

⅓ cup olive oil

1 tablespoon red wine vinegar

2 tablespoons maple syrup

1 teaspoon Dijon mustard

½ teaspoon dried oregano

salt and pepper to taste

Whisk together oil, vinegar, maple syrup, mustard, oregano, salt and pepper until well blended.

Betsy Cozine, Atlanta, GA

Thai Salad

¾	cup olive oil
½	cup sugar
⅓	cup vinegar
1	12-ounce package broccoli slaw mix
1	cup slivered almonds, roasted
1	cup sunflower seeds
1	bunch green onions, finely chopped
2	packages oriental flavored Ramen noodles, uncooked

Combine oil, sugar, vinegar, slaw mix, almonds, sunflower seeds and green onion and refrigerate overnight. Before serving, stir in crushed uncooked noodles.

Noodles can be toasted before adding to salad.

June Rose, Atlanta, GA

Janet Sunshine, Atlanta, GA

Warm Bean and Onion Ring Salad

1	2.8-ounce can French fried onions
2	tablespoons Dijon style mustard
2	tablespoons cider vinegar
2	shallots, minced
½	cup olive oil
	salt and pepper to taste
2	pounds fresh green beans, ends trimmed

Crisp onion rings on baking sheet in preheated 350 degree oven for 7 to 10 minutes. Turn oven off but leave onions inside to keep warm. Whisk together mustard and vinegar in small saucepan. Mix in shallots and slowly whisk in olive oil. Season with salt and pepper. Bring mixture to boil, whisking constantly, then cook 2 minutes. Keep warm over low heat. Cook beans in large pot of boiling water just until crisp-tender, 4 to 5 minutes. Drain and immediately transfer to mixing bowl. Toss with warm dressing; mix in toasted onions. Serve immediately.

Serves 9

Poppy Seed Dressing

⅔	cup sugar
1	teaspoon dry mustard
1	teaspoon paprika
½	teaspoon salt
⅓	cup honey
3	tablespoons lemon juice
3	tablespoons vinegar
2	teaspoons grated onion
1	cup salad oil
1	tablespoon poppy seeds

Mix together sugar, mustard, paprika and salt. Add honey, lemon juice, vinegar and onion; stir. Pour into blender; cover and blend on high speed 1 minute. Remove cover and, while running, slowly pour in oil through opening. Pour into container and stir in poppy seeds.

Makes 1 pint

This dressing does not separate.
Mickey Sachs

Poultry and Seafood

HOSPITALITY

Chicken Artichoke Casserole

3	cups diced chicken breast
2	14-ounce cans artichoke hearts
1	cup mayonnaise
1	tablespoon lemon juice
1	6-ounce jar sliced mushrooms
2	10¾-ounce cans cream of chicken soup
½	teaspoon curry powder
1	8-ounce can sliced water chestnuts
1½	cups grated cheese
1¼	cups plain breadcrumbs

Grease 3 quart casserole dish with butter. Put in layer of chicken and then layer of artichoke hearts. Repeat. Combine mayonnaise, lemon juice, mushrooms, soup, curry powder and water chestnuts and pour over layers. Top with cheese and breadcrumbs. Bake in preheated 350 degree oven for 25 minutes.

Serves 12

Can substitute tuna for chicken.
Elizabeth Neal, Rome, GA

Chicken Strips with Prosciutto

2	pounds thin sliced boneless chicken breast
½	cup flour
1	teaspoon salt
½	teaspoon black pepper
¼	cup olive oil
¼	cup unsalted butter
1	cup diced onion
6	ounces prosciutto, sliced in 1x½ inch strips
1	pound sliced mushrooms
½	cup dry Marsala wine

Cut chicken breasts into 2x3 inch strips. Combine flour, salt and pepper. Dredge each chicken piece in flour mixture. Heat oil over medium heat and add butter. Sauté chicken until golden brown and remove. Add onion and cook until soft. Add prosciutto, stirring constantly, for 2 minutes; add mushrooms, stirring constantly for 1 minute. Return chicken to pan and add wine. Turn heat up to high and stir constantly for 2 minutes to reduce wine.

Serves 6 to 8

Tracey Wallace, Roswell, GA

Chicken and Corn Chili

2	tablespoons vegetable oil
4	garlic cloves, minced
2	red or yellow peppers, cored and chopped
1	large onion, chopped
1½	tablespoons chili powder
1	teaspoon ground cumin
¼	teaspoon cayenne pepper, or to taste
1	14½-ounce can diced tomatoes
1	13¾-ounce can chicken broth
1	pound boneless, skinless chicken breasts cut into ½ inch pieces
1	15½-ounce can black beans, drained and rinsed
¾	cup prepared salsa
1½	cups frozen whole corn kernels
½	teaspoon black pepper
¼	teaspoon salt, or to taste

Heat oil in large heavy pot. Add garlic, peppers and onion. Sauté 5 minutes, stirring frequently. Add chili powder, cumin and cayenne. Cook 1 minute, stirring constantly. Add tomatoes and broth. Bring mixture to boil. Reduce heat to medium low, simmer for 15 minutes, or until slightly thickened, stirring occasionally. Stir in chicken, beans, salsa and corn. Cover and bring to boil. Reduce heat to medium and simmer for 5 minutes, or until chicken is cooked through. Stir in black pepper and salt.

Serves 4 to 6

Suzanne Bible, Atlanta, GA

Chicken Marsala

¼ cup flour
¼ teaspoon salt
¼ teaspoon pepper
1 teaspoon dried basil
4 boneless, skinless chicken breast halves, about 1¼ pounds
3 tablespoons olive oil, divided
1 tablespoon butter
2 garlic cloves, finely chopped
2 cups sliced or quartered mushrooms
1 tablespoon dried parsley flakes
¾ cup dry Marsala wine or chicken broth

Mix flour, salt, pepper and basil well in shallow dish or plate. Wrap a chicken breast in plastic wrap and pound to approximately ¼ to ½ inch uniform thickness using the smooth side of meat mallet. Remove breast from plastic wrap and coat well with flour mixture; shake off excess. Repeat with remaining 3 breasts. Heat oil and butter in 10 to 12 inch skillet over medium high heat. Cook chicken fillets in pan until coating is golden brown and crispy; remove chicken from skillet and set aside. In the same skillet, cook garlic, mushrooms and parsley in remaining oil for 5 minutes, stirring frequently and scraping brown bits from bottom of pan. Add wine to skillet and cook until reduced by half, about 5 minutes. Add the chicken back to skillet; cover and cook for 5 to 8 minutes more, or until chicken is no longer pink in center.

Serves 4

David Lundy, Atlanta, GA

Chicken Tetrazzini

1	16-ounce package vermicelli
½	cup chicken broth
4	cups chopped, cooked chicken breasts
1	10¾-ounce can cream of chicken soup
1	10¾-ounce can cream of celery soup
1	8-ounce carton sour cream
1	6-ounce jar sliced mushrooms, drained
½	cup shredded Parmesan cheese
1	teaspoon pepper
½	teaspoon salt
2	cups shredded Cheddar cheese

Prepare vermicelli according to package directions; drain. Return to pot and toss with chicken broth. Stir together cooked chicken, chicken soup, celery soup, sour cream, mushrooms, Parmesan cheese, pepper and salt in a large bowl; add vermicelli and toss well. Spoon mixture into 2 lightly greased 11x7 inch baking dishes. Sprinkle evenly with Cheddar cheese. Cover and bake in preheated 350 degree oven for 30 minutes; uncover and bake 5 minutes more or until cheese is melted and bubbly.

Serves 12

Freeze unbaked casserole up to 1 month. Thaw overnight in refrigerator, let stand 30 minutes at room temperature and bake as directed.

Susan Taulman, Atlanta, GA

Spicy Thai Chicken

2	tablespoons olive oil
2	garlic cloves, chopped
1	medium onion, sliced
3-4	skinless, boneless chicken breasts, sliced
1	14-ounce can light coconut milk
1	teaspoon Thai red curry paste, or more to taste
1	8-ounce can sliced water chestnuts
1	14-ounce jar roasted red peppers, sliced
1	tablespoon chopped cilantro, or more to taste
1	ripe avocado, sliced
	cooked rice or egg noodles

Heat oil over medium heat in large skillet. Add garlic and onion and sauté. Add chicken and cook until almost cooked through. Add coconut milk and curry paste and stir until combined. Simmer 5 minutes. Add water chestnuts and red peppers. Simmer 5 minutes. Add cilantro and stir. Serve in bowls over rice or egg noodles. Garnish with sliced avocado and cilantro sprig.

Julie Mitchell, Atlanta, GA

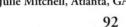

Poulet à la Moutarde
Chicken with Mustard

1	3½ to 4-pound chicken, skin and backbone removed and cut into 8 pieces
	salt and pepper to taste
¼	teaspoon dried thyme
	Dijon mustard
	flour for dredging
4	tablespoons butter, divided
1	onion, finely chopped
½	cup dry white wine
½	cup chicken stock
½	pound mushrooms, sliced
1	cup frozen pearl onions
¼	cup water
½	cup heavy cream
¼	cup finely chopped parsley
	cooked rice or noodles

Rub chicken with salt, pepper and thyme and coat liberally with mustard. Cover with foil and refrigerate overnight. The next day dredge chicken in flour and sauté in 2 tablespoons butter until brown. Remove and set aside. In same pan, sauté onion. Put chicken and onion in a deep casserole dish; add wine and stock. Cover and cook over low heat for 45 minutes or until chicken is done. Meanwhile, in separate saucepan, sauté mushrooms in 1 tablespoon butter; remove from pan and set aside. In the same pan, sauté pearl onions in 1 tablespoon butter and water until onions are soft. Mix in mushrooms and set aside. When ready to serve, skim fat from the cooked chicken. Add cream and bring to simmer. If not thick enough, add small amount of cornstarch which has been dissolved in small amount of cold water. Add onion and mushroom mixture. Correct seasonings, sprinkle with parsley and serve with rice or noodles.

Serves 4

Recipe can be doubled and reheats well.

Aline Callahan, Chamonique, France and Atlanta, GA

TORTILLA CHICKEN

12 corn tortillas

1 10¾-ounce can cream of chicken soup

1 10¾-ounce can cream of mushroom soup

1 cup milk

1 onion, grated

1 4-ounce can green chilies, cut into small pieces

2 tablespoons chicken broth

4 cups cooked diced chicken

2 cups grated Cheddar cheese

Cut tortillas into quarters. Mix soups, milk, onion and green chilies. Grease 9x12 inch baking dish and pour chicken broth in bottom of dish. Place in dish a layer of tortillas, layer of chicken, layer of soup mix; repeat layers. Top with grated cheese. Refrigerate overnight. Bake in preheated 300 degree oven for 1 hour or until bubbling.

Serves 8

Jean T. Gregory,
Atlanta, GA

QUICK CHICKEN LIVERS

¼ cup butter

1 pound chicken livers

2 tablespoons chopped parsley

2 tablespoons finely chopped green onion

1 garlic clove, finely chopped

2 tablespoons flour

2 tablespoons red wine

2 tablespoons red wine vinegar

salt and pepper to taste

Melt butter in skillet over medium heat. Add chicken livers and sauté until no longer red. Add parsley, green onion and garlic. Sprinkle flour over liver mixture and cook until flour is brown. Add wine and vinegar. Cover and simmer over low heat for 5 minutes. Add salt and pepper and serve.

This recipe is wonderful served over rice pilaf.

Sharon Tatom,
Tucson, AZ

Sautéed Ashley Farm Chicken Breast with Wild Mushroom Sauce

	olive oil for sautéing
2	chicken breasts
	salt and pepper to taste
2	shallots, minced
2	cups mushrooms, cleaned and trimmed
1	cup white wine
4	cups chicken stock
½	cup heavy cream (optional)
2	tablespoons sweet butter (optional)
	sautéed spinach

Heat olive oil in sauté pan. Season chicken with salt and pepper. Place chicken skin or smooth side down in pan. Cook on medium high heat until golden brown on both sides. Remove pan from heat. Remove chicken from pan and place in baking dish. Bake in preheated 350 degree oven until done. Place pan back on medium heat. Add shallots and cook briefly. Add mushrooms and cook until just tender. Season with salt and pepper. Add white wine and reduce until pan is almost dry. Add chicken stock and reduce to ½ cup. If desired, finish with heavy cream and stir in butter. To assemble, cover bottom of platter with sautéed spinach. Place chicken on spinach. Spoon sauce over chicken.

Hilary White, Executive Chef, 103 West, Atlanta, GA

Savory Chicken Squares

1	3-ounce package cream cheese
3	tablespoons melted butter, divided
2	cups cooked chicken or 10 ounces canned chicken, drained
½	teaspoon salt
⅛	teaspoon pepper
1	tablespoon chopped onion
2	tablespoons milk
1	8-ounce can crescent rolls
	breadcrumbs for topping

In medium bowl, blend cream cheese and 2 tablespoons melted butter. Add chicken, salt, pepper, onion and milk and mix well. Separate crescent dough into 4 rectangles, firmly pressing perforations to seal. Spoon ½ cup chicken mixture onto center of each rectangle, pull 4 corners to top and seal edges. Brush top with remaining butter, sprinkle with breadcrumbs and bake on ungreased cookie sheet in preheated 350 degree oven for 20 to 25 minutes.

Serves 4

Joan Ventresea, Atlanta, GA

Early Spring Pasta

Oriental Dressing
1   large onion, sliced
1¼   cups water, divided
¼   cup soy sauce
¼   cup rice vinegar
1   tablespoon minced garlic
1   tablespoon minced gingerroot
1   tablespoon sesame oil
1   tablespoon lemon juice
1½   teaspoons sugar
1½   teaspoons hot pepper sauce
2   tablespoons cornstarch

Pasta
½   pound turkey breast cut into julienne strips
¼   pound carrots cut into julienne strips
¼   pound asparagus, diagonally sliced into 1 inch pieces
¼   pound fresh spinach, chopped
¾   pound linguine, cooked and drained

To prepare dressing, spread onion in large baking pan. Cook in preheated 400 degree oven until edges are dark brown, about 15 minutes. Process onion in food processor until smooth. Place onion, 1 cup water, soy sauce, rice vinegar, garlic, ginger, oil, lemon juice, sugar and pepper sauce in medium saucepan and bring to boil. Combine cornstarch with remaining water and stir until smooth; gradually stir into dressing mixture. Heat until mixture boils, stirring constantly. Reduce heat to low; simmer 2 to 3 minutes. Bring mixture to boil and add turkey, carrots, asparagus and spinach; reduce heat to medium. Cook 2 to 3 minutes. Pour sauce over linguine and toss gently to coat.

Serves 4 to 6

Carol Sharkey, Atlanta, GA

Turkey Tetrazzini

½ pound vermicelli
6 tablespoons butter
2 tablespoons flour
1 cup cream
2 cups chicken broth
  salt, pepper and nutmeg to taste
3 tablespoons dry sherry
½ pound mushrooms, sliced
5 cups turkey or chicken, chopped
½ cup black olives, sliced
½ cup Parmesan cheese

Cook vermicelli according to package directions; drain. Melt butter in pan; stir in flour until combined. Add cream and broth, stirring until combined. Stir in salt, pepper, nutmeg and sherry. Mix ½ the sauce with mushrooms and vermicelli and pour into buttered 3 quart casserole. Mix remaining sauce with turkey or chicken and olives and pour over pasta. Top with Parmesan cheese and bake in preheated 350 degree oven for 20 minutes.

Serves 10

Shirley Heermann, Atlanta, GA

Turkey Vegetable Loaf

1½ pounds ground turkey
½ cup shredded carrots or ½ cup chopped green pepper
1 9-ounce package frozen or fresh spinach
1 cup rolled oats
1½ tablespoons Italian seasoning
1 egg or 2 egg whites
¼ cup milk
  salsa

In large bowl, mix together turkey, carrots or green pepper, spinach, oats, Italian seasoning, egg and milk. Shape mixture into loaf and place in greased 2 quart casserole dish. Cover and bake in preheated 375 degree oven for 50 minutes. Remove cover and bake 10 minutes until juices run clear. Slice and serve with salsa.

Alida V. Coles, Conyers, GA

Linguine with Clams

½	pound linguine
3	garlic cloves
3	tablespoons olive oil
12-16	littleneck clams
1	tablespoon flour
½	cup dry white wine
1	tablespoon lemon juice
	red pepper flakes to taste
2	tablespoons finely chopped Italian parsley

Two 6½-ounce cans of undrained baby clams can be substituted for the littleneck clams and white wine. The sauce will not need additional salt because the clams will add the saline component.

Cook linguine according to package directions; drain and reserve 1 cup pasta water. Peel and lightly crush garlic cloves with side of knife, being sure to leave them whole. Cook in olive oil in sauté pan over medium heat until golden. Add clams and flour. Cover pan and cook for 5 to 7 minutes, checking from time to time to remove any clams as soon as they open to prevent overcooking. Remove clams from shells and set aside. Add wine and lemon juice to pan and continue cooking over medium heat a few more minutes. Add pepper flakes and stir to combine. Add pasta, clams and parsley to sauce and stir to mix, adding a little pasta water if needed. Heat thoroughly and serve, garnishing with additional sprinkling of parsley.

Andrea Johnson, Atlanta, GA

Similar recipe contributed by Mary Stephens, Alpharetta, GA

Oysters Rockefeller Casserole

This recipe can be cut in half and baked in 1½ quart casserole dish at 350 degrees for 30 minutes. It can also be frozen after cooking and reheated.

2	tablespoons anise seeds
2	cups water
4	10-ounce packages frozen chopped spinach
½	teaspoon salt
¼	teaspoon pepper
¼	teaspoon cayenne pepper
½	tube anchovy paste
8	bacon strips, cooked and cut into pieces
½	cup butter, divided
1	cup chopped celery
1½	cups chopped green onions
1	garlic clove, crushed
1	teaspoon thyme
1	cup chopped parsley
1	tablespoon Worcestershire sauce
2	pints oysters, drained, reserving ½ cup liquid
½	cup oyster liquid
1½	cups seasoned breadcrumbs, divided
½	cup grated Parmesan cheese

Simmer anise seeds in 2 cups water for 8 to10 minutes. Discard seeds. Cook spinach in remaining water. Add salt, pepper and cayenne. When spinach is done, drain well. Add anchovy paste and bacon pieces. Set aside. In large skillet, melt ¼ cup butter over medium heat. Add celery, onion, garlic and thyme. Sauté for 5 minutes. Add parsley and Worcestershire and stir until hot, about 2 minutes. Drain liquid and set aside. In another skillet, cook oysters in ½ cup oyster liquid and remaining butter until oysters curl, about 3 minutes. Add enough breadcrumbs, about 1 cup, to absorb liquid and continue heating until hot. Breadcrumbs and oysters will look like oatmeal mush. Set this mixture aside. In large bowl mix spinach mixture, celery mix and oyster mix. Pour into greased 3 quart casserole dish. Top with remaining breadcrumbs and Parmesan cheese. Bake in preheated 350 degree oven for 30 minutes. Serve as main dish or as side with roast turkey or baked ham.

Serves 12 to 15

Elizabeth Neal, Rome, GA

Crab au Gratin

White Cream Sauce
½ cup butter to clarify
½ cup flour
2 cups milk
2 cups heavy cream
2 tablespoons diced onion
½ teaspoon salt
   white pepper to taste

Crab au Gratin
2   pounds jumbo lump blue crabmeat
2   tablespoons cooking oil
1   cup dry sherry
3   cups white cream sauce (above)
1   teaspoon salt
2   cups grated white Cheddar cheese
12 slices white bread
4   whole lemons

To prepare cream sauce, melt butter in small saucepan and skim off white foam. Allow to cool slightly and pour clarified butter into small bowl. Discard white milk solids left in pan. Return butter to saucepan with flour and whisk together. Heat until bubbling and whisk in milk and cream. Reduce heat to low simmer and add onion, salt and white pepper. Simmer while stirring frequently for 10 minutes and strain through wire mesh soup strainer to remove onion. To prepare gratin, make sure that all shells have been removed and crabmeat is still in lumps. Sauté crabmeat in oil in large sauté pan. When hot, add sherry to deglaze and reduce until liquid is almost gone. Add cream sauce and bring to simmer. Season with salt. Preheat oven to high temperature (preferable use broiler). Divide crab mixture equally between 8 gratin dishes and smooth down lumps; top with cheese. Remove bread crusts and cut each piece in half diagonally. Place on baking sheet and toast on both sides under broiler (or bake in high temperature oven until lightly browned). Place gratin dishes under broiler and allow top to brown. Serve with 3 toast points and ½ lemon.

Serves 8
Piedmont Driving Club, Atlanta, GA

"Shepherd Center has given me the foundation to get my life back. I am completely confident that it's just a matter of time and patience, but I know I can have my life back."

Tara Robertson,
former SCI patient

Crab Cakes

Crab Cake Mayonnaise
1   cup mayonnaise
1½   teaspoons Worcestershire sauce
5   drops hot pepper sauce
1   teaspoon Old Bay seasoning
1½   teaspoons dry mustard
¼   teaspoon salt
2   tablespoons fresh lemon juice

Crab Cake Mix
½   cup chopped green onions
2   tablespoons olive oil
1   pound jumbo lump crabmeat
1   whole egg
1   cup cracker crumbs
     additional cracker crumbs for breading

To prepare mayonnaise mixture, combine mayonnaise, Worcestershire, pepper sauce, Old Bay seasoning, dry mustard, salt and lemon juice. Set aside. To prepare crab mix, sauté green onion in olive oil until soft. Chill completely. Combine green onion, crabmeat, egg, cracker crumbs and mayonnaise mixture in bowl; mix well. Scoop into 3 ounce portions, roll in cracker crumbs and form into cakes. Sauté in olive oil over medium heat until golden brown on both sides. Bake in preheated 350 degree oven for 5 minutes to heat thoroughly.

J. Kevin Walker, CMC, Cherokee Town & Country Club, Atlanta, GA

Fish Saltimbocca Style

2   halibut filets, skinless
3   prosciutto slices, very thin
4   sage leaves
2   tablespoons flour
     salt and pepper to taste
     olive oil

Top one side of fish with layer of prosciutto and 2 sage leaves, securing sage with toothpick. Dredge fish in flour mixed with salt and pepper. Heat enough olive oil to coat nonstick pan over medium heat. Add fish with prosciutto side down. Cook approximately 4 minutes; turn and cook another 2 to 3 minutes, depending on thickness of fish. Carefully remove toothpicks before serving.

This recipe has been adapted from Vitello alla Saltimbocca (veal scaloppini topped with prosciutto and sage), a very popular dish in Rome.

Andrea Johnson, Atlanta, GA

Deviled Crab

¼ cup butter
½ cup chopped onion
1 teaspoon flour
1   cup milk
1 pound crabmeat
1 teaspoon salt
1 teaspoon balsamic vinegar
1 tablespoon lemon juice
½-1 teaspoon cayenne pepper
    cracker crumbs or seasoned breadcrumbs

Mix butter, onion, flour, milk, crabmeat, salt, vinegar, lemon juice and cayenne and place in crab shells or large ramekins. Sprinkle with cracker crumbs or breadcrumbs and dot with additional butter. Bake in preheated 350 degree oven for 30 to 40 minutes.

Serves 8

Neale Bearden, Atlanta, GA

Heavenly Broiled Fish

½ cup grated Parmesan cheese
¼ cup butter, softened
3 tablespoons mayonnaise
3 tablespoons chopped green onion
¼ teaspoon salt
    hot pepper sauce to taste
2 pounds fish filets, skinless
3 tablespoons lemon juice

Combine cheese, butter, mayonnaise, green onion, salt and pepper sauce. Set aside. Place filets in single layer on well greased broiler pan. Brush filets with lemon juice. Broil 4 inches from flame for 4 to 6 minutes. Remove from broiler and place cheese mixture over each filet. Broil 2 minutes or until lightly browned.

Serves 6

Jan Andrews, Atlanta, GA

Red Snapper Livornese

4	tomatoes, coarsely chopped
2	bell peppers, seeded and chopped
1	small onion, chopped
1	garlic clove, finely chopped
4	tablespoons extra virgin olive oil
12	calamata olives, pitted and halved
1	tablespoon capers
2	pounds red snapper filets
	salt to taste
	breadcrumbs

Sauté tomatoes, bell pepper, onion and garlic in olive oil 18 to 20 minutes until soft. Add olives and capers. Set aside. Sprinkle red snapper lightly with salt and breadcrumbs. Bake at 400 degrees for 16 to 20 minutes. Be careful not to overcook. Pour sauce over fish and serve.

Serves 4

Suzanne Inman, Atlanta, GA

"Your Favorite Fish" Hong Kong Style

Soy Broth

½	cup light soy sauce
¼	cup water
⅓	cup dry sherry wine
2	tablespoons sugar

Fish

2	8-ounce portions of your favorite fish, white, light, flaky fish is suggested
1	pound fresh spinach, washed and stemmed
2	tablespoons sesame oil
2	tablespoons olive oil
	salt and pepper to taste
2	tablespoons finely julienned ginger
2	tablespoon finely julienned scallions
	cooked rice

To prepare broth, combine soy sauce, water, wine and sugar and bring to boil. Steam or sauté fish. Sweat spinach in sesame and olive oils and season with salt and pepper. For plate presentation, place bed of spinach in soup bowl, rest fish on top of spinach and garnish with ginger and scallions. Pour broth over fish and serve with sticky rice and chopsticks.

Serves 2

Robert Holley, Executive Chef, Atlanta Fish Market, Atlanta, GA

Never Fail Fancy Company Salmon

4	5 to 6-ounce salmon filets, skinless
	salt and pepper to taste
¼	cup lemon butter dill sauce, divided
1	bunch fresh dill weed
3	bell peppers, julienned
2	tablespoons chopped onion
½	cup shredded carrots
2	teaspoons olive oil
2	tablespoons lime juice
1	lime, sliced

Rinse salmon and dry with paper towel; season with salt and pepper. Place salmon in flat container and spread 2 teaspoons lemon butter dill sauce over each filet. Cover with plastic wrap and refrigerate for 30 minutes. Reserve 4 sprigs of dill and chop the rest. Set aside. Combine bell pepper, onion and carrots in olive oil in quart container and microwave on high for 3 minutes. Drain and set aside. Cut parchment paper in 14 inch sections and oil one side. Remove salmon from refrigerator and put each filet on piece of parchment paper. Add another teaspoon of dill sauce to each and top with teaspoon chopped fresh dill and ¼ vegetable mixture. Sprinkle lime juice over each filet. Fold parchment paper and seal ends. Place packets on baking pan, seam side down, and bake in preheated 425 degree oven for 18 to 20 minutes. Remove salmon from packets, garnish with dill sprigs and lime slice.

This salmon recipe is a good, easy way to get Omega 3 with nice flavor and crispy vegetables.

Karen Shepherd Spiegel, Atlanta, GA

SALMON MARINADE

⅓ cup soy sauce
½ cup fresh lemon juice
1 garlic clove, minced
1 tablespoon Dijon mustard
2 tablespoons dried parsley
1 tablespoon ground ginger
3-4 salmon filets
cooked rice

Combine soy sauce, lemon juice, garlic, mustard, parsley and ginger. Marinate salmon filets for 15 minutes or overnight. When ready to serve, place salmon and marinade in dish and bake in preheated 350 degree oven for 30 to 40 minutes or until cooked to desired doneness. Salmon can also be grilled. Serve with rice and top with marinade.

Ansley Conner, Atlanta, GA

Thai Salmon

1	large onion, sliced thick
2	large tomatoes, sliced thick
4	salmon filets
12-16	fresh basil leaves
4	tablespoons Thai chili sauce
	pepper to taste

In bottom of large rectangular baking dish lay onion slice and then tomato slice on top of onion. Lay salmon on top of tomato so that filet completely covers tomato. Lay basil leaves on filet, one leaf at a time, until entire filet has been covered. Spoon sauce on filet, but don't cover completely. Sprinkle with pepper. Repeat layers for each filet. Cover dish with aluminum foil and bake in preheated 400 degree oven for 30 minutes. If additional time is needed for cooking, remove aluminum foil and continue cooking until desired doneness.

Great served with horseradish mashed potatoes and a salad. This dish is easy to prepare and has a great taste.

Debbie Gross, Atlanta, GA

Shrimp Daufuskie

½	pound bacon, chopped
1½	cups chopped onions
4	large celery ribs, chopped
1	large green bell pepper, seeded and chopped
2	garlic cloves, chopped
1	12-ounce bottle seafood cocktail sauce
2	15½-ounce cans diced tomatoes
2	jalapeño peppers, seeded and chopped (optional)
2	pounds shrimp, peeled and deveined
	hot pepper sauce (optional)
	cooked rice

In large skillet over medium heat, fry bacon crisp. Set aside. Discard all but 2 tablespoons fat. Sauté onion, celery, bell pepper and garlic in fat for 8 to 10 minutes until soft. Add cocktail sauce and stir. Add 1 can undrained tomatoes and 1 can drained tomatoes. Stir. Add crumbled bacon and jalapeños. Simmer 1 hour. Add shrimp just before serving and cook 5 minutes. Add pepper sauce for more spice. Serve over rice.

Serves 8

Alana Shepherd, Atlanta, GA

SALMON CHEESE CASSEROLE

2½ cups seasoned small croutons

1 16-ounce can salmon, flaked and deboned

2 cups grated sharp Cheddar cheese

4 eggs

2 cups milk

½ teaspoon Worcestershire sauce

½ teaspoon dry mustard

1 teaspoon salt

Layer ½ croutons, ½ salmon and ½ cheese in greased 1½ quart casserole dish. Repeat layer. Beat eggs and stir in milk, Worcestershire, mustard and salt. Pour over salmon mixture. Bake in preheated 350 degree oven for 40 to 50 minutes until knife comes out clean in center.

Marilyn Cates, Atlanta, GA

Shrimp Floridian

1	8-ounce package cream cheese
1	cup bleu cheese
1	8-ounce carton sour cream
2	tablespoons finely chopped garlic
4	tablespoons chopped parsley
½	cup dry white wine
2	pounds shrimp, peeled, deveined and cooked
1	lemon, thinly sliced
	cooked wild rice
	paprika

Blend together cream cheese, bleu cheese and sour cream, being careful to get a smooth mixture. Add garlic and parsley and mix well. Add wine, being careful not to make mixture too thin. Place shrimp in baking dish and top with cheese sauce and lemon slices. Cover and bake in 300 to 325 degree oven for 15 minutes, or until lemon slices are tender. Do not let mixture bubble up. Serve over wild rice, top with lemon slices and garnish with parsley and paprika.

Serves 6

For variation, instead of wild rice, use 6 baked potatoes quartered. Place on serving dish and spoon shrimp mixture over potatoes, top with lemon slice and garnish with parsley and paprika.

Nancy Montgomery, Atlanta, GA

Grilled Marinated Shrimp

1	pound large shrimp
1	cup olive oil
3	garlic cloves, minced
1	tablespoon minced onion
3	teaspoons sugar
2	teaspoons salt
1	teaspoon pepper
1	teaspoon grated ginger
½	teaspoon cumin
2	tablespoons lemon juice

Peel and devein shrimp. Set aside. For marinade, combine olive oil, garlic, onion, sugar, salt, pepper, ginger, cumin and lemon juice. Add marinade to shrimp and refrigerate for 5 to 24 hours. Grill shrimp for 2 minutes on each side.

The grilled shrimp may be used as main course and served over rice or as appetizer.

Doris Shelton, Atlanta, GA

Jambalaya

1½	pounds boneless, skinless chicken breast cut into 2 inch chunks
2½	teaspoons salt, divided
½	teaspoon pepper
¼	teaspoon dried thyme leaves
2	tablespoons olive oil
1	cup chopped yellow onion
½	cup chopped celery
½	cup chopped green bell pepper
½	cup chopped red bell pepper
½	teaspoon cayenne pepper
2	tablespoons chopped garlic cloves
2	links Andouille sausage, cut into ¼ inch slices
1½	cups uncooked, converted long-grain white rice
1	8-ounce can tomato sauce
2½	cups chicken broth
½	cup dry white wine
1	bay leaf
½	pound shrimp, peeled and deveined
½	cup chopped green onions

In small bowl, toss chicken with 1 teaspoon salt, pepper and thyme to coat evenly. Set aside. In large saucepan, heat oil over medium heat. Stir in onion, celery, green and red bell peppers, remaining salt and cayenne. Sauté vegetables until onions are translucent, 4 to 6 minutes. Stir in garlic, sausage and seasoned chicken. Cook, stirring occasionally, for 8 minutes. Stir in rice, tomato sauce, broth, wine and bay leaf and bring to boil. Reduce heat to medium low. Cook covered, stirring every 5 minutes to avoid burning, until rice is tender and liquid is absorbed, about 23 to 27 minutes. Stir in shrimp. Remove pan from heat; let stand covered for 2 to 3 minutes. Remove bay leaf and sprinkle with green onions to serve.

Serves 6

Chicken thighs will also work well in this recipe. Add chili powder for more spice.

Debi Cziok, Atlanta, GA

Mrs. Reardy's Shrimp and Artichokes

1	14-ounce can artichoke hearts, not marinated, drained
2	6½-ounce cans jumbo lump crabmeat or 1 pound fresh crabmeat
1	pound fresh medium shrimp, shelled, deveined and cooked
½	pound fresh mushrooms, sliced
6½	tablespoons butter, divided
4½	tablespoons flour
1½	cups half & half
1	tablespoon Worcestershire sauce
¼	cup very dry sherry wine
	salt and white pepper to taste
¼	cup freshly grated Parmesan cheese
	cooked rice
	fresh parsley, chopped

Quarter artichokes and arrange in 3 quart greased glass baking dish. Pick over crabmeat and remove any shell or cartilage. Spread shrimp and crabmeat over artichokes. Do not break up lumps of crabmeat. Sauté mushrooms in 2 tablespoons butter for 5 minutes. Arrange evenly over seafood. In large heavy skillet, melt remaining butter and blend in flour. Cook and stir for 3 to 5 minutes. Slowly add half & half, stirring constantly until thickened and smooth. Add Worcestershire, wine, salt and pepper. Mix well and pour over ingredients in casserole dish. Sprinkle with cheese and bake in preheated 375 degree oven for 20 minutes. Do not overcook as casserole will be watery. Serve over rice and sprinkle with parsley.

Serves 6 to 8

Mrs. Reardy was the housekeeper for Adlai Stevenson when he served as U. S. Ambassador to the United Nations. When Mrs. Reardy served this casserole to President John F. Kennedy as a guest, he requested the recipe.

Joan Brown, Atlanta, GA

Spicy Curried Shrimp with Thin Spaghetti

1	teaspoon grated lemon zest
2	tablespoons lemon juice
3	tablespoons tamari sauce
3	tablespoons red curry paste
2	tablespoons sugar
1	tablespoon chili or canola oil
1	pound medium shrimp, peeled, deveined and cut in half lengthwise
1	cup diced yellow, orange or red bell pepper
⅓	cup thinly sliced scallions
2	tablespoons finely chopped cilantro
½	pound thin spaghetti, cooked and drained, reserving ½ cup cooking liquid
	vegetable cooking spray
4	teaspoons chopped cashew nuts

For marinade, combine lemon zest, lemon juice, tamari sauce, curry paste, sugar and oil in small bowl and mix well. Place shrimp in another bowl and add ½ of marinade. Cover bowl and marinate for 40 minutes, with 30 minutes in refrigerator and 10 minutes at room temperature. Add remaining marinade to bell pepper, scallions, cilantro and cooked spaghetti. Set aside. Spray oil on large skillet and sauté shrimp until tender, 4 to 5 minutes. Add shrimp to pasta mixture and toss well. Add reserved pasta cooking liquid if dish becomes too dry. Garnish with nuts.

Serves 4

Scallops with Pasta in Baked Tomato Sauce

8	ripe Roma tomatoes, cut into thin wedges
6	fresh basil leaves, chopped
2-3	garlic cloves, minced
2	tablespoons extra virgin olive oil, divided salt and pepper to taste
1	pound sea scallops, tough side and muscles removed
1	16-ounce package penne pasta

Place ½ the tomatoes in greased small baking dish. Scatter ½ the basil and garlic over tomatoes, drizzling 1 tablespoon oil and seasoning with salt and pepper. Lay scallops on tomatoes and repeat another layer of tomatoes, basil and garlic, remaining oil, salt and pepper. Bake in preheated 400 degree oven about 30 minutes or until tomatoes are very soft. Cook pasta according to directions; drain and transfer to serving dish. Top with baked tomato-scallop mixture and toss well. Serve immediately.

Serves 6

Meat and Game

HOSPITALITY

Baked Stuffed Onions

4	large onions
1	pound ground beef or sausage
¼	pound margarine
¼	cup chopped parsley
2½	cups water, divided
1	8-ounce package cornbread stuffing mix
2	chicken bouillon cubes

Peel onions and cut in half crosswise. Remove center of onions, leaving about ½ inch shell. Chop center of onion, making 2 cups. In large skillet over medium heat, cook chopped onion and meat, stirring to break up meat. Add margarine, parsley and 1 cup water; cook until margarine melts. Stir in cornbread stuffing mix. Spoon stuffing into onion shells, mounding mixture high and smoothing to edge. Place onions in baking pan; dissolving bouillon cubes in remaining water and add to pan. Bake loosely covered with foil in preheated 350 degree oven for 1 hour and 15 minutes or until onion shells are tender. Baste once with pan liquid.

Serves 4 to 8

Mary Ellen Sherman, Atlanta, GA

Beef Chunks in Burgundy

1½	pound round steak or lean beef stew meat, cut in 1 inch cubes
2	teaspoons salt
	freshly ground pepper to taste
2	tablespoons butter
1	medium onion, chopped
1	cup sour cream
1	cup grated Cheddar cheese
½	cup Burgundy wine
1	garlic clove, minced
¼	teaspoon thyme
¼	teaspoon marjoram
¼	teaspoon basil
1	10¾-ounce can cream of mushroom soup
	cooked rice or pasta

Season beef cubes with salt and pepper. Place butter in skillet over medium heat. Add beef cubes and brown all sides. Add onion near the end of browning time and cook until soft. Transfer beef mixture to large casserole dish and add sour cream, cheese, wine, garlic, thyme, marjoram and basil. Cover and bake in preheated 325 degree oven for 2 hours or until meat is almost tender. Add soup; mix well and bake for an additional 20 minutes. Serve over rice or pasta.

Serves 6

Mattie Lisenby, Atlanta, GA

Beef à la Deutsch
"Company Casserole"

1	6-ounce package wide noodles
1	cup sour cream
1	cup cottage cheese
1	bunch green onions including tops, chopped olive oil or butter for browning
1	pound ground beef
1	6-ounce can tomato sauce salt, pepper, minced garlic and oregano to taste fresh grated Parmesan cheese to taste

Cook noodles in boiling water until al dente. Place ½ of noodles in bottom of large baking dish. Combine sour cream, cottage cheese and onion and pour over mixture. Top with remaining noodles. Place olive oil or butter in skillet and brown ground beef. Pour off drippings. Add tomato sauce, salt, pepper, garlic and oregano to beef. Cook on medium heat for 30 minutes. Add beef mixture on top of noodle mixture. Top with Parmesan cheese and bake in preheated 350 degree oven for 30 minutes or until bubbly.

Serves 10

This recipe is even better when reheated the next day.
Dorothy Thrower, Tyler, TX

Beef Brisket

¾	cup ketchup, divided
1	package onion soup mix, divided
1	5-pound beef brisket
1	cup water

Crisscross heavy foil in bottom of roasting pan so brisket can be enveloped and sealed tightly. Pour in ½ of ketchup and ½ package onion soup mix. Lay brisket, fat side up, on top of ketchup mixture. Pour remaining ketchup and remaining onion soup mix on top of brisket. Add water and seal. Cook for 3 to 3½ hours. Check at 2 hours to make sure there is enough liquid; you may want to add another ½ cup water. Transfer to carving board and cool for ½ hour. Carve across grain and arrange in pan, overlapping slices slightly. Pour defatted juices over top and refrigerate overnight. Reheat in preheated 325 degree oven for 15 to 20 minutes.

Ann Levin, Atlanta, GA

Beef Stroganoff

¼ cup butter
¼ cup thinly sliced onions
1 garlic clove, minced
½ pound sliced fresh mushrooms
1½ pounds ground sirloin or round steak
3 tablespoons lemon juice
3 tablespoons red Burgundy wine
1 10½-ounce can beef consommé
1 teaspoon salt
¼ teaspoon black pepper
¼ pound small noodles
1 8-ounce carton sour cream
  parsley (optional)

Melt butter in large skillet over medium heat. Sauté onion, garlic and mushrooms. Add beef and cook until red color disappears. Stir in lemon juice, wine, beef consommé, salt and pepper; simmer uncovered for 15 minutes. Stir in uncooked noodles. Cook covered for 5 minutes. Stir in sour cream. Garnish with parsley, if desired.

Marian Stevens, Atlanta, GA

Pot Roast

1 3-pound bottom round rump roast
2 teaspoons salt
1 teaspoon pepper
1 teaspoon oregano
1 teaspoon dill
2 bay leaves
1 tablespoon dry mustard
2 tablespoons olive oil
½ cup water
1 medium onion, halved
¼ cup dry red wine
  small new potatoes cut in half
  carrots, peeled and cut into chunks
  onions, peeled and cut into wedges

Season roast with salt, pepper, oregano, dill, bay leaves and dry mustard. In Dutch oven, heat olive oil and sear roast on medium heat until well browned. Add water and halved onion. Cover and cook in preheated 300 degree oven for 3 hours. Check at intervals to turn roast and to add wine. During the last 45 minutes, add new potatoes, carrots and onion wedges.

Lanie Jones Wilson, Atlanta, GA

Brunswick Stew

A SHORTER BRUNSWICK
STEW RECIPE

3 cups chicken broth

**2½ cups chopped
cooked chicken**

**1 24-ounce container
barbeque shredded pork**

**1 16-ounce package frozen
vegetable gumbo mixture**

**1 10-ounce package
frozen corn**

**1 10-ounce package
frozen petite lima beans**

½ cup ketchup

Bring all ingredients to
boil in Dutch oven over
medium high heat, stirring
often. Cover and reduce
heat to low; simmer,
stirring occasionally,
for 25 minutes or until
thoroughly heated.

Serves 8 to 10

4	boneless, skinless chicken breast halves
4	bay leaves
4	celery stalks with leaves
3½	quarts water
1½	teaspoons salt
2	teaspoons hot pepper sauce
2	medium onions, chopped
1	16-ounce package whole kernel corn
1	16-ounce package frozen lima beans
2	28-ounce cans crushed tomatoes, undrained
1	pound ground beef
1	pound cooked barbeque chopped pork
½	cup Worcestershire sauce
2	teaspoons garlic salt
2	teaspoons dried oregano
2	teaspoons allspice
2	teaspoons ground black pepper
1	teaspoon cayenne pepper
1½	teaspoons liquid smoke

Combine chicken, bay leaves, celery, water, salt and pepper sauce in large stock pot over medium heat and cook uncovered for 1 hour. Remove chicken, cool and chop. Save all broth, discarding bay leaves and celery. Add onion, corn, beans and tomatoes to broth. Bring to boil and cook for 15 minutes; reduce heat and simmer for 1 hour, stirring often. Brown ground beef in skillet, crumbling beef as you cook. Drain off all fat. Add beef, chicken, pork, Worcestershire, garlic salt, oregano, allspice, pepper, cayenne and liquid smoke to stew. Simmer uncovered for 1 hour, stirring occasionally.

Makes 6 quarts

This recipe makes a large quantity; you may want to freeze some for later.
Carol Dew, Atlanta, GA

Lasagna

2	tablespoons vegetable oil
1	pound ground beef
¾	cup chopped onion
1	16-ounce can tomatoes
2	6-ounce cans tomato paste
2	cups water
2	tablespoons chopped parsley
2	teaspoons salt
1	teaspoon sugar
1	teaspoon garlic powder
½	teaspoon pepper
½	teaspoon oregano leaves
1	8-ounce box lasagna noodles
1	16-ounce carton ricotta cheese
2	cups shredded mozzarella cheese
1	cup grated Parmesan cheese

Heat oil in large, heavy pan over medium heat and lightly brown beef and onion. Add tomatoes, stirring to break up, and tomato paste, water, parsley, salt, sugar, garlic powder, pepper and oregano leaves. Simmer uncovered, stirring occasionally for about 30 minutes. At the same time, cook lasagna noodles as directed and drain. In 13x9x2 inch baking pan, spread about 1 cup of beef sauce and alternate layers of lasagna noodles, beef sauce, ricotta, mozzarella and Parmesan cheese, ending with beef sauce, mozzarella and Parmesan cheese. Bake in preheated 350 degree oven for 40 to 50 minutes or until lightly browned and bubbling. Let stand for 15 minutes; cut into squares to serve.

Serves 8

Claire Smith, Atlanta, GA

Marinated Beef Tenderloin

5-8	pounds beef tenderloin
	coarsely ground pepper or lemon pepper to taste
2	garlic cloves, crushed
1½-2	cups soy sauce
½-¾	cup bourbon
3-4	bacon strips
1	medium onion, sliced

Place roast in large plastic bag. Sprinkle with pepper. Mix together garlic, soy sauce and bourbon and pour into bag over roast. Marinate at room temperature for 2 hours or overnight in refrigerator. Allow roast to come to room temperature before roasting. Remove roast from marinade, place in roasting pan on rack, pour marinade over roast and top with bacon and onion slices. Place in preheated 450 degree oven and immediately reduce temperature to 400 degrees. Cook for 35 to 50 minutes until meat thermometer reads 135 degrees.

Becky Maddox, Atlanta, GA

Meat Loaf

1½	pounds ground round
⅓-½	pound ground veal or lamb
1	egg
4	tablespoons ketchup
6	tablespoons Worcestershire sauce
½	small yellow onion, chopped
½	large green pepper, chopped
½	cup Italian style breadcrumbs
	salt and pepper to taste
	steak sauce

In a large bowl, mix ground round, veal or lamb, egg, ketchup, Worcestershire, onion, pepper, breadcrumbs, salt and pepper. Put in 9x5 inch loaf pan. Cover meat loaf with steak sauce and bake in preheated 350 degree oven for 1 hour. Meat thermometer should read 160 degrees when done.

Peggy Conner, Atlanta, GA

Marinated London Broil with Béarnaise Sauce

Marinated London Broil

2½	pounds London broil
⅓	cup vinegar
1	teaspoon dried oregano
1	teaspoon dried basil
1	teaspoon dried sage
1	teaspoon dried thyme
1	teaspoon dried rosemary
1	bay leaf
1	teaspoon hot pepper sauce
1	teaspoon minced garlic
½	onion, minced
1	egg yolk
1	cup olive oil
	salt and freshly ground pepper to taste

Béarnaise Sauce

1	shallot, minced
2	teaspoons dried tarragon
2	tablespoons wine vinegar
2	tablespoons white wine
3	egg yolks
1	cup plus 2 tablespoons butter, melted
1	teaspoon lemon juice
	hot sauce and Worcestershire sauce to taste
	salt and ground pepper to taste

To prepare meat, place meat in a shallow baking dish or large plastic bag. Combine vinegar, oregano, basil, sage, thyme, rosemary, bay leaf, pepper sauce, garlic, onion, egg yolk, oil, salt and pepper and pour over meat. Cover meat and refrigerate overnight, turning once or twice. Grill, turning once after 7 to 8 minutes for rare. To prepare sauce, combine shallot, tarragon, vinegar and wine in small saucepan and bring to boil over high heat. Reduce heat and simmer until almost evaporated. At the same time, place egg yolks in metal pan over simmering water and using a whisk, stir until the yolks are thickened. Add melted butter, 1 or 2 drops at a time, stirring with a whisk after each addition until all butter is incorporated. Remove egg yolk mixture from heat. Add lemon juice, hot sauce, Worcestershire, salt, pepper and shallot mixture to egg yolk mixture. Slice London broil and serve with Béarnaise sauce.

Joane Askins, Atlanta, GA

Southwestern Meat Loaf

1	pound ground round
1	cup frozen corn
1½	cups picante sauce
1⅓	cups rolled oats
¼	cup minced fresh cilantro
1	tablespoon chili powder
1½	teaspoons ground cumin
1	large egg white
¼	cup ketchup

Combine ground round, corn, picante sauce, oats, cilantro, chili powder, ground cumin and egg white in large bowl and stir well. Shape ground round mixture into 9x5 inch loaf pan coated with cooking spray. Place loaf pan on baking sheet and brush top with ketchup. Bake in preheated 375 degree oven for 50 minutes. Let meat loaf stand for 10 minutes before slicing.

To prepare meat loaf in advance, shape ground round mixture into loaf, wrap in heavy duty plastic wrap and freeze. Thaw overnight in refrigerator; bake as directed above.

New England Beef Stew

3-4	pounds marbleized chuck roast, cut into bite size pieces
	flour for dredging
	Montreal seasoning salt to taste
1	tablespoon vegetable oil
1	large onion, chopped
1	10½-ounce can beef broth
1	14-ounce can chicken broth
3-4	baking potatoes, peeled and cubed
1½	cups mini carrots, peeled
⅓	cup potato flakes

Sprinkle roast pieces with flour and Montreal seasoning salt. Heat oil in Dutch oven; add onion and sauté for about 2 minutes on medium heat. Add roast and brown all sides. Add beef broth and chicken broth. Cover and place in preheated 350 degree oven for 1 hour. Add potatoes and carrots. Cover and cook for additional 20 minutes. Add potato flakes to thicken.

Serves 4 to 6

This recipe is best when using Montreal seasoning salt rather than a substitute.

Lucy T. Inman, Atlanta, GA

Old Atlanta Beef Stew

4	bacon strips, diced
3	pounds lean beef, cut into 2 inch chunks
16	pearl onions
5	large carrots (cut into ¾ inch slices)
2	bay leaves
½	teaspoon thyme
½	teaspoon rosemary
2½	cups dry red wine
	beef broth
1	cup frozen peas
2½	teaspoons cornstarch
2½	teaspoons water
	salt and pepper to taste
	cooked rice or pasta

Place bacon strips in 6 quart Dutch oven and cook over medium heat for 5 minutes. Add beef chunks, turning until browned. Stir in onion, carrots, bay leaves, thyme, rosemary and wine and bring to boil. Reduce heat and cover. Cook until beef is tender, about 3 hours. Remove meat and vegetables from Dutch oven. Skim fat and discard. Measure oven juices and add enough beef broth to make 2 cups. Return meat and vegetables to oven, stir in peas and bring to boil. Reduce heat, dissolve cornstarch in water and stir into Dutch oven stirring constantly until sauce thickens. Add salt and pepper. Serve with rice or pasta.

Serves 6 to 8

Cile Stockhausen, Atlanta, GA

Onion-Hamburger Casserole

¾	pound ground beef
2	14½-ounce cans whole tomatoes, drained, reserving ¼ cup juice
1	medium Vidalia onion, chopped
1	2-ounce can sliced pimento, divided
1	3-ounce can sliced mushrooms, drained
½	package onion soup mix
1	small red bell pepper, diced
¾	teaspoon salt
¼	teaspoon pepper
1	large can refrigerator biscuits
6	medium Vidalia onions, sliced and divided
1	cup grated Cheddar cheese

Place beef in skillet over medium high heat and cook until browned. Drain fat from beef and add tomatoes, chopped onion, ½ pimento, mushrooms, onion soup mix, bell pepper, salt and pepper. Line bottom and sides of 12 inch glass dish with biscuits in 3 separate layers. Lay 3 sliced onions on top of biscuits. Pour beef mixture on top of onions and pour reserved tomato juice on top of beef mixture. Place remaining sliced onions on top. Cover dish with aluminum foil and cook in preheated 375 degree oven for 50 minutes. Remove from oven and sprinkle with cheese and remaining pimiento. Place back in oven and bake for an additional 10 minutes.

Serves 8 to10

Mary Ellen Sherman, Atlanta, GA

Sauerbraten

Sauerbraten

3-3½	pounds beef round or rump roast
1	teaspoon salt
½	teaspoon pepper
4	bay leaves
½	teaspoon peppercorns
8	whole cloves
2	medium onions, sliced
1	small carrot, minced
1	stalk celery, chopped
1½	cups red wine vinegar
2½	cups water
¼	cup butter

Gingersnap Gravy

1½	cups hot marinade
2	tablespoons sugar
½	cup water
⅔	cup gingersnap crumbs (approximately 8 gingersnaps)
	salt to taste

To prepare Sauerbraten, thoroughly rub meat with salt and pepper. Place in deep earthenware dish or ovenware glass bowl with bay leaves, peppercorns, cloves, onion, carrot and celery. Heat vinegar and water to boiling in saucepan over high heat and pour over meat. Let cool, cover well and refrigerate at least 48 hours, turning meat twice a day. Remove meat from marinade, dry with towels and reserve marinade. Melt butter in Dutch oven or skillet over medium heat. Add meat and brown on all sides. Strain solids from reserved marinade and pour over meat. Cover and simmer for 2½ to 3 hours or until tender. Remove meat to warmed serving platter. To prepare gravy, bring reserved marinade to a boil; stir in sugar, water, crumbs and salt and heat thoroughly. Slice meat and serve with gravy.

Serves 6

Must prepare in advance.

Sunday Afternoon Beef Short Ribs

Marinade

	olive oil for sautéing
2	onions, sliced
1	leek, sliced (whites and pale green parts only)
2	carrots, peeled and sliced
3	plum tomatoes, chopped
8	garlic cloves
4	sprigs fresh thyme
8	sprigs flat leaf parsley
4	bay leaves
3	cups dry red wine

Ribs

4	pounds beef short ribs, 2 inches thick and cut into pairs
	salt and pepper to taste
	olive oil for sautéing
5	cups beef stock

To prepare marinade, heat large saucepot over medium heat and add oil. Sauté onion, leek and carrots until lightly browned. Add tomatoes, garlic, thyme, parsley, bay leaves and red wine. Simmer for 10 minutes and cool to room temperature. To prepare ribs, trim ribs of excess fat and place in marinade. Refrigerate overnight (8 hours minimum). Remove ribs from marinade and reserve marinade. Pat dry with clean kitchen towel. Season generously with salt and pepper. Heat large braising pot over high heat and add oil. Brown ribs and add reserved marinade (make sure the bones are facing up). Bring to simmer and add beef stock and bring back to a simmer. Cover and bake in preheated 350 degree oven. Begin to test for doneness after 1½ hours by inserting paring knife into meat; knife should encounter little resistance and meat should nearly fall off bone. When tender, remove ribs from liquid and strain into saucepan. (Save vegetables and enjoy). Skim excess fat and reduce liquid until slightly thickened. Season with salt and pepper. Place ribs meat side up and return to oven and bake at 450 degrees for an additional 10 minutes until nicely glazed. Pour reduced sauce over ribs and serve.

Serves 4

Gary Donlick, Executive Chef, Pano's and Paul's, Atlanta, GA

Stuffed Flank Steak

1½	pounds flank steak
2	slices white bread
½	pound fresh mild Italian sausage
1	10-ounce package frozen spinach, thawed and drained
2	eggs
2	tablespoons olive oil
2	garlic cloves, minced
¾	cup Parmesan cheese
	salt to taste

Cut or have butcher cut a pocket in long side of steak being careful not to make holes. In large bowl, moisten bread with water and squeeze dry. Mix bread with sausage, spinach, eggs, oil, garlic, cheese and salt. Place steak in baking pan. Carefully stuff sausage mixture into steak pocket. Lace opening together with cooking twine. Bake in preheated 300 degree oven for 1½ to 2 hours. Chill overnight. Slice and serve.

For hors d'oeuvres, slice into ¼ inch pieces, cut each in half and serve with crackers. This is great for picnics.

Dianne Isakson, Marietta, GA

Rosemary Lamb Lollipop with Fig Balsamic Compote

	salt and pepper to taste
1	tablespoon chopped garlic
1	tablespoon chopped rosemary
6	tablespoons olive oil
1	rack Australian lamb (10 to 12 ounces)
1	cup balsamic vinegar
¼	cup honey
½	cup sun-dried figs, stems removed

In large bowl, combine salt, pepper, garlic, rosemary and olive oil and season lamb. Combine balsamic vinegar with honey and figs in saucepan and simmer over low heat until fig mixture is reduced to syrup consistency. Place fig mixture in blender and blend until smooth. Roast lamb in roasting pan in preheated 400 degree oven and cook for about 20 minutes for medium rare. Remove lamb from oven and let stand for 10 minutes. Cut lamb into individual lamb chops. Place dollop of fig compote onto each lamb lollipop. Serve warm.

Tony Conway, Owner, and Christophe Holmes, Executive Chef, A Legendary Event, Atlanta, GA

Lamb Pilaf

4 tablespoons butter or margarine, divided
3 pounds boned lamb, cut in 1 inch cubes
1 large onion, thinly sliced into rings
½ teaspoon cinnamon
½ teaspoon ground pepper
2 cups uncooked rice, divided
1 cup golden raisins, divided
2 teaspoons salt
1 10½-ounce can beef consommé
2 cups water
¼ cup lemon juice
1 cup sliced almonds, toasted
3 tablespoons chopped parsley

Melt 2 tablespoons butter or margarine in large skillet. Sauté half of lamb over high heat until browned. Remove lamb to large bowl lined with paper towels. Drain excess fat from pan. Repeat with remaining lamb. Lower heat to medium and sauté onion, cinnamon and pepper in same skillet for about 3 to 5 minutes. Lightly butter a 2½ quart casserole dish. Layer rice, raisins, meat, and onion in casserole dish. Repeat, making three layers. Sprinkle top with salt. Combine consommé and water and pour over casserole dish. Cover and bake in preheated 400 degree oven for 50 minutes. Uncover, sprinkle with lemon juice and almonds and bake an additional 10 minutes uncovered. Garnish with parsley before serving.

Serves 6 to 8

Roasted Colorado Rack of Lamb with Natural Jus

Rack of Lamb
2   racks Colorado Lamb
     chopped garlic cloves
     sea salt and fresh ground black pepper to taste

Lamb Stock
10   pounds lamb bones
2   large onions, chopped
4   large carrots, chopped
1   head large celery, chopped
4   large tomatoes, chopped
2   cups tomato paste
2   gallons cold water
4   bay leaves
1   bunch fresh thyme
     sea salt and fresh ground black pepper to taste
     peppercorns to taste
2   tablespoons butter

To prepare lamb, rub racks of lamb with chopped garlic, salt and pepper. Marinate over night in refrigerator. Take lamb out of refrigerator and sear all sides in large skillet over medium high heat. Roast in a preheated 400 degree oven and cook for about 20 minutes for medium rare. To prepare stock, roast lamb bones with onion, carrots, celery and tomatoes for 1 hour, adding tomato paste during the last ½ hour. Deglaze stock with cold water scraping bottom of pan to remove small bits. Add bay leaves, thyme, salt, pepper and peppercorns, bring to a slight simmer and simmer until stock is reduced to ⅓. Strain stock through a fine sieve and season to taste. Top with butter right before serving.

This recipe can be served with or without the stock.

Tony Conway, Owner, and Christophe Holmes, Executive Chef, A Legendary Event, Atlanta, GA

Enchiladas Suisas

Salsa Verde (Green Chile Sauce)
2   tablespoons butter
⅔   cup chopped Spanish onion
2   tablespoons flour
1½   cups chicken broth
1   cup canned chopped green chiles, or more to taste
1   large garlic clove, finely minced
¾   teaspoon salt
        dash of ground cumin

Enchiladas
12   corn tortillas
        vegetable oil
1   cup grated Monterey Jack cheese
1   cup grated mild Cheddar cheese
2   cups cooked chicken or pork, grated
1   cup heavy cream
¼   cup chopped scallions, including tops
        pimiento-stuffed olives, sliced
        cherry tomatoes, sliced

To prepare sauce, melt butter in a saucepan over medium heat. Add onion and sauté until soft. Stir in flour and add broth. Add chiles, garlic, salt and cumin. Reduce heat and simmer for 15 minutes. Set aside. To prepare enchiladas, heat oil in a heavy skillet over medium high heat. Lightly fry tortillas in oil being careful not to crisp the tortillas. Combine cheeses and reserve ½ cup. Dip each tortilla (both sides) in Salsa Verde. Place 2 heaping tablespoons chicken or pork and 2 tablespoons cheese mixture in the center of each tortilla. Roll tortillas and place seam side down in 13x9x2 inch baking dish. Spoon additional sauce over tortillas and pour heavy cream evenly over tortillas. Sprinkle with reserved cheese mixture and scallions. Bake in preheated 350 degree oven uncovered for 20 minutes. Serve immediately, garnished with olives and cherry tomatoes. Any left over Salsa Verde can be served on the side.

Serves 8 to 10

This dish is inexpensive, beautiful and easy. A family favorite.

Florence Inman, Atlanta, GA

Overnight Lasagna

1	pound sweet Italian sausage, casings removed
4	cups prepared spaghetti sauce
1	cup water
1	15-ounce carton ricotta cheese
2	tablespoons chopped fresh chives
½	teaspoon oregano leaves
1	egg
1	8-ounce box uncooked lasagna noodles
1	16-ounce package sliced mozzarella cheese
2	tablespoons Parmesan cheese

In large skillet, brown sausage and drain well. Add spaghetti sauce and water and blend well. Simmer on low heat for 5 minutes. In medium bowl, combine ricotta cheese, chives, oregano and egg. Mix well. In bottom of ungreased 13x9x2 inch baking dish or lasagna pan, spread 1½ cups meat sauce, top with ½ uncooked noodles, ½ ricotta cheese mixture and ½ mozzarella cheese. Repeat with remaining noodles, ricotta cheese mixture and mozzarella cheese and top with remaining meat sauce. Sprinkle with Parmesan cheese, cover and refrigerate overnight. Bake uncovered in preheated 350 degree oven for 50 to 60 minutes or until noodles are tender and casserole is bubbly. Remove from oven and let stand for 15 minutes before serving.

Serves 12

Carol Sharkey, Atlanta, GA

Pork Tenderloin with Cinnamon

2	pounds pork tenderloin
4	tablespoons sugar
¼	teaspoon salt
4	tablespoons soy sauce
¼	teaspoon cinnamon
2	tablespoons sherry
1	teaspoon powered ginger
2	teaspoons dry mustard
2	teaspoons lemon juice

Place pork in roasting pan. Combine sugar, salt, soy sauce, cinnamon, sherry, ginger, mustard and lemon juice and pour over pork. Bake in preheated 350 degree oven for 1 hour, basting frequently with sauce.

Serves 4 to 6

This recipe is good as a main course or thinly sliced on rolls for hors d'oeuvres.
Ann Williams, Atlanta, GA

Pork Tenderloin with Caramelized Apples

1¼	pounds pork tenderloin
2	tablespoons Dijon mustard
1	tablespoon chopped fresh sage
	salt and pepper to taste
3	Golden Delicious apples, peeled and cut into 16 wedges
¼	cup maple syrup

Place pork in shallow baking pan coated with cooking spray. Combine mustard and sage in a small bowl. Rub tenderloin with salt and pepper and spread the mustard mixture on all sides. Bake in preheated 450 degree oven for 25 minutes or until meat thermometer registers 160 degrees. While pork is baking, heat heavy cast iron or nonstick skillet over medium high heat. Add apples and sauté for 5 minutes or until lightly browned. Reduce heat to low and add maple syrup. Simmer for 10 additional minutes or until apples are tender, stirring occasionally. Cut pork crosswise into slices; serve with cooked apples.

Serves 4

Beth Taquechel, Atlanta, GA

Spinach and Bacon Stuffed Pork

½ cup finely chopped onion
1-2 garlic cloves, minced
1 cup sliced fresh mushrooms
1 10-ounce package frozen spinach, thawed and drained
4 bacon strips, cooked and crumbled
3 tablespoons Dijon mustard, divided
½ teaspoon salt, divided
1¼ teaspoons pepper, divided
2 ¾-pound pork tenderloins or a 1½ pound pork loin
2 teaspoons dried rosemary, crushed
1 teaspoon dried oregano
1 teaspoon dried thyme
½ cup Chablis wine

Cook onion and garlic in skillet coated with cooking spray on medium heat, stirring until tender. Add mushrooms and cook an additional 3 minutes. Stir in spinach, bacon, 1 tablespoon mustard, ¼ teaspoon salt and ¼ teaspoon pepper and set aside. Slice pork lengthwise but not all the way through. Cover pork with plastic wrap and pound into 12x8 inch rectangle. Spoon spinach mixture over pork to within ½ inch of side. Roll pork in jelly-roll fashion starting with the short sides. Tie with cooking twine at 1½ inch intervals. Combine remaining mustard, rosemary, oregano, thyme, remaining salt and pepper. Spread over tenderloins. Place pork seam down in roasting pan coated with cooking spray. Add wine to pan. Bake in preheated 325 degree oven for 45 minutes. Take pork out of oven and let stand for 10 minutes. Slice and serve.

Serves 6

Mary Kay Howard, Marietta, GA

Hungarian Veal Casserole

½   cup butter, divided
4   pounds veal, cubed
    salt and pepper to taste
3   10¾-ounce cans cream of mushroom soup, undiluted
3   cups sliced onions
¼   cup water
¼   teaspoon seasoned salt
    dash of hot pepper sauce
⅓   cup sherry
1   cup sour cream

Melt ¼ cup butter over medium heat in large skillet. Add veal cubes and cook until veal is browned. Remove veal from skillet and place in large casserole dish with cover. Sprinkle veal with salt and pepper and cover with mushroom soup. Melt remaining butter over medium heat in skillet. Sauté onion until golden brown and spoon over veal. Combine water, seasoned salt and pepper sauce in skillet over high heat, bring to a boil and scrape to remove brown pieces in bottom of pan. Spoon mixture over veal. Bake covered in preheated 375 degree oven for 40 minutes. Add sherry and bake an additional 30 minutes uncovered. Add sour cream and stir until blended. Bake an additional 10 minutes uncovered.

Serves 8 to10

Cubed beef or lamb could be substituted for the veal in this recipe.
Carol Sharkey, Atlanta, GA

Veal Marsala

1   pound veal scaloppini, ¼ inch or less thick
    flour, salt and pepper for dredging
¼   cup olive oil
3   tablespoons butter
¼   cup beef broth
2   garlic cloves, minced
1   cup Marsala wine or more to taste, divided

Dredge veal in flour, salt and pepper. Heat oil and butter in skillet on medium heat and fry veal. Reduce heat; add beef broth, garlic and ½ cup wine. Cover skillet and simmer for 10 minutes. Remove veal, scrape away flour and place veal steaks on a warm platter. Add remaining wine to skillet, increase heat to high and reduce by ½. Strain liquids and pour over veal steaks.

Serves 4

Use genuine Sicilian Marsala wine, preferably sweet.
Charles Craig, Atlanta, GA

Osso Bucco

6-8 large veal shanks, cut 2½ inches thick (about 3 pounds)
  salt and pepper to taste
  flour for dredging
3 tablespoons olive oil (or more)
7 tablespoons butter (or more), divided
1½ cups dry white wine
1½ cups finely chopped onion
¾ cup finely chopped carrots
¾ cup finely chopped celery
1½ teaspoons minced garlic
4 cups beef broth
1½ cups chopped plum tomatoes
1 Bouquet garni (6 parsley sprigs, 4 thyme sprigs, 1 bay leaf)
  wrapped in cheesecloth

Gremolata is a garnish made of minced parsley, lemon zest and garlic. It is sprinkled over Osso Bucco and other dishes to add a fresh, sprightly flavor.

Gremolata: Stir together the following:

½ cup minced parsley

2 tablespoons lemon zest

1 tablespoon minced garlic

Season veal with salt and pepper and dredge in flour. Heat oil and 3 tablespoons butter in heavy skillet over moderate high heat. Brown veal, adding more butter if necessary. Remove veal from skillet, add wine to skillet and boil until reduced to ½ cup. Reserve. Add remaining 4 tablespoons butter to large flame proof casserole dish and cook onion, carrots, celery and garlic over moderate low heat until softened. Add veal shanks and any accumulated juices to casserole dish. Add reserved wine and enough broth to almost cover the veal. Spread tomatoes on top of veal. Add salt and pepper to taste; add bouquet garni and bring to simmer over moderate high heat. Cover and place in preheated 325 degree oven for 3 hours. Transfer veal to ovenproof serving dish and keep warm. Strain pan juices into saucepan, pressing hard on the solids. Bring pan juices to boil, reducing to about 3 cups, about 15 minutes. Baste veal shanks in the reduced juices and bake for an additional 10 minutes, basting 3 more times. Pour juices over shanks and serve. Serve remaining juices in a gravy boat.

Serves 4

Pat Monaco, Smyrna, GA

Stuffed Loin of Veal with
Porcini Mushrooms and Barolo Wine Sauce

2	pounds veal loin
1	pound porcini mushrooms
2	eggs
1	cup breadcrumbs
1	cup chopped fresh Italian parsley
1	sprig fresh thyme
	salt and pepper to taste
2	ounces chopped truffles (optional)
	oil for searing
⅓	cup brandy
1¾	cups Barolo wine
½	cup cream

Remove skin from veal loin and trim. Place loin in a roasting pan and make an incision in center of veal loin. Combine mushrooms, eggs, breadcrumbs, parsley, thyme, salt and pepper in food processor and process until smooth; add truffles, if using. Using pastry bag, fill veal loin with mixture. Close ends of loin with cooking twine and sear all sides in hot oil. Bake in preheated 375 degree oven for 20 minutes. Remove loin from pan, add brandy and Barolo wine to hot roasting pan. Stir over medium heat until reduced by ½ and add cream. Deglaze for 5 minutes; pour glaze over veal and serve.

Serves 6

Sergio Favalli and Chef Antonio Abizanda, La Grotta Ristorante Italiano, Atlanta, GA

White Collops

A Highland version of Veal Scallops

1½	pounds veal cutlets, thinly sliced
	flour for dredging
¼	cup butter
1	cup chicken stock or bouillon
½	teaspoon grated lemon zest
⅛	teaspoon mace
1	cup sliced mushrooms, if desired
	salt and pepper to taste

Pound cutlets between sheets of waxed paper until very thin and dredge in flour. Melt butter in heavy saucepan and sauté veal on both sides until golden brown, adding more butter if necessary. Add stock or bouillon, lemon zest, mace, mushrooms, salt and pepper. Cover tightly and cook for 30 to 45 minutes or until meat is tender. Thicken gravy as desired.

Serves 4 to 6

Jan Ruane, Glasgow, Scotland

Dove with Marsala Wine

½	cup butter
14-20	doves
½	cup olive oil
1	tablespoon seasoned salt
1	tablespoon garlic powder
4	dashes of Worcestershire sauce
	pepper to taste
¾	cup Marsala wine
3	tablespoons flour
1	cup warm water
3	2¾-ounce packages quick cooking wild rice

In pot large enough to hold dove covered with liquid, melt butter over medium heat. Place dove in butter and brown. While browning, add seasoned salt, garlic powder, Worcestershire and pepper. Remove dove when browned and deglaze pan with wine. Simmer for 3 minutes. Dissolve flour in water and add to wine a little at a time, stirring to prevent lumps. Cover pot tightly and simmer on medium to low heat for 45 minutes to 1 hour, stirring occasionally. Add additional water if needed for desired gravy consistency. Cook wild rice according to directions on package and serve dove on bed of rice.

Serves 8

You may want to add watercress sprigs for garnish.

Charles T. Pottinger III, Atlanta, GA

Quail with White Wine

1	cup flour for dredging
	salt and pepper to taste
½	cup butter or margarine, melted
12	quail, cleaned
8	ounces fresh mushrooms, sliced
1	10¾-ounce can cream of mushroom soup, undiluted
1	cup dry white wine
	cooked wild rice

In a large bowl, season flour with salt and pepper. Melt butter in large skillet over medium high heat; dredge quail in flour and brown. Remove quail and place in large casserole with lid. Add mushrooms, soup and wine to skillet to form gravy; if not enough gravy, add a little warm water and stir well. Pour gravy over quail and bake covered in a preheated 350 degree oven for 1 hour. Test for tenderness. Serve with wild rice.

Serves 6 to 8

Charles T. Pottinger III, Atlanta, GA

Pot Roast of Venison

½	cup flour
1	roast of venison, 2 inch thick
3	tablespoons vegetable oil
¼	cup chopped celery
1	turnip, chopped
3	tablespoons chopped onion
½	teaspoon salt
	freshly ground coarse black pepper to taste
1	cup boiling water, divided
1¼	cups dry red wine, divided

Pound flour into venison. Heat oil in large heavy pan over medium heat, add venison and cook until browned. Add celery, turnip, onion, salt, pepper and 1/2 cup water and ¾ cup wine. Reduce heat and simmer covered for at least 1 hour. (Be sure lid is tight as steam is necessary to tenderize meat.) Add remaining water and wine and continue to simmer until tender.

You can substitute carrot for turnip.

Serve with sliced lemon and brandied fruit.

Charles T. Pottinger III, Atlanta, GA

Vegetables and More

HOSPITALITY

Vegetables and More

Lemon Spaghetti

⅔ cup olive oil
⅔ cup freshly grated Parmesan cheese
½ cup fresh lemon juice
½ teaspoon salt
½ teaspoon freshly ground black pepper
1 pound dried spaghetti
⅓ cup chopped fresh basil
1 tablespoon grated lemon zest

In large bowl, whisk oil, Parmesan cheese, lemon juice, salt and pepper to blend. Cover and refrigerate for up to 8 hours. Bring to room temperature before using. Cook spaghetti in large pot of boiling water, stirring occasionally until tender, about 8 minutes. Drain, reserving 1 cup of cooking liquid. Add spaghetti to lemon sauce and toss with basil and lemon zest. Toss pasta with enough reserved cooking liquid ¼ cup at a time to moisten. Season pasta with more salt and pepper to taste. Transfer to bowl and serve.

Joane Askins, Atlanta, GA

Orzo Parsley Gratin

1 pound orzo pasta
6 garlic cloves, unpeeled
1 cup heavy cream
1 cup chicken broth
1 cup grated Parmesan cheese, divided
1¼ cups minced fresh parsley, divided
    salt and pepper to taste
4 tablespoons dry breadcrumbs
3 tablespoons unsalted butter

In boiling, salted water, cook orzo and garlic for 10 minutes; drain. Rinse under cold water and drain. Remove garlic, peel and mash with fork. In large bowl, whisk garlic with cream; add orzo, broth, ¾ cup Parmesan cheese, 1 cup parsley, salt and pepper and mix well. Spoon into buttered 2 quart baking dish and smooth top. Toss breadcrumbs with remaining parsley and Parmesan cheese and sprinkle evenly over pasta. Dot with butter cut into very thin slices. Bake in preheated 325 degree oven for 1 hour 15 minutes or until bubbly and top is golden.

Serves 10

May be made a day ahead and kept refrigerated.

Alana Shepherd, Atlanta, GA

"Shepherd Center did everything they could to get me ready to return home so that I can do the every day activities that I need to do."

Robert Sneller,
former SCI patient

Pesto Provençal

1	pound dried spinach fettuccine
4	cups fresh basil leaves
½	cup olive oil
½	cup freshly grated Parmesan cheese
3	garlic cloves, peeled
½	teaspoon salt
1	cup crumbled feta cheese
¼	cup toasted pine nuts

Bring large pot of water to rapid boil. Add pasta and cook until al dente. Drain and rinse with hot water; drain. While pasta cooks, place basil, oil, Parmesan cheese, garlic and salt in blender. Blend, pulsing and scraping down the sides as needed, until pesto becomes consistency of grains of sugar. Toss pesto and pasta and fold in feta. Top with pine nuts and serve.

Dean Melcher, Atlanta, GA

Yorkshire Pudding

2	cups flour, sifted
1	teaspoon salt
2	cups milk, or 1 cup light cream and 1 cup milk
4	eggs
8	teaspoons fat from roast or bacon drippings

Sift together flour and salt in bowl. Slowly stir in milk and then beat vigorously until smooth. Add eggs, one at a time, beating for 1 minute with rotary beater after each addition to make creamy batter. Cover bowl with dry towel and chill batter for at least 2 hours. Spoon fat from roast into shallow pan and put in oven until drippings are sizzling hot. Beat chilled batter vigorously several times and pour to about ½ inch depth into hot pan. Bake in preheated 450 degree oven for 15 minutes. When pudding has risen, reduce temperature to 350 degrees and bake for 10 to 15 minutes, until light, crisp and brown. Cut pudding into squares, put on a hot platter and serve with roast and gravy.

Serves 6

Marian Taulman Bales, Gallantin Gateway, MT

Au Gratin Potatoes

1	30-ounce package frozen hash browns
½	cup butter, melted
½	cup chopped onions
1	10¾-ounce can cream of chicken soup
2	cups sour cream
1	teaspoon salt
½	teaspoon pepper
2	cups grated sharp Cheddar cheese
1	cup crushed cornflakes

Thaw potatoes and mix together with butter, onion, soup, sour cream, salt, pepper and cheese. Spoon into greased 9x13 inch baking dish. Sprinkle with cornflakes; cover and bake in preheated 350 degree oven for 45 minutes; uncover and bake 15 minutes.

May be cooked ahead and heated before serving.

Carol Thompson, Atlanta, GA

Golden Parmesan Potatoes

¼	cup flour
¼	cup grated Parmesan cheese
¾	teaspoon salt
⅛	teaspoon pepper
6	large red potatoes, peeled and cut into eighths
⅓	cup melted butter
2	tablespoons chopped fresh parsley

Combine flour, cheese, salt and pepper in paper or plastic bag. Moisten potatoes with water, place in bag, 8 to 10 pieces at a time, and shake, coating potatoes well. Pour melted butter into 13x9 inch pan and place potatoes in pan forming a single layer. Bake in preheated 375 degree oven for 60 minutes, turning potatoes once midway through baking. Sprinkle with fresh parsley.

Serves 6 to 8

Lois Puckett, Atlanta, GA

Similar recipe submitted by Carol Crichton, Atlanta, GA

CHARMENT'S MACARONI AND CHEESE

5 12-ounce packages Stouffer's Macaroni and Cheese, thawed

2 eggs, beaten

1 jigger sherry

2 cups grated sharp Cheddar cheese, divided

In large bowl, mix macaroni and cheese, eggs, sherry and 1½ cups cheese. Pour macaroni and cheese mixture into greased 2 quart casserole dish. Sprinkle with remaining cheese and bake in preheated 350 degree oven for 1 hour.

Serves 10 to 12

Cover macaroni and cheese with aluminum foil while baking if edges get too brown.

Gloria Stone, Avondale Estates, GA

Potatoes Gruyère

6	large baking potatoes
½	cup butter, divided
	salt and ground pepper to taste
1¼	cups grated Gruyère cheese, divided
¾	cup whipping cream

Bake potatoes and let cool. Scoop out potatoes and place in bowl. Coarsely chop potatoes and place half in 8 or 9 inch glass baking dish. Dot with 4 tablespoons butter and sprinkle with salt and pepper and ½ the cheese; repeat with second layer. Pour cream over top and refrigerate overnight. Bake in preheated 375 degree oven for 20 to 30 minutes or until a golden crust has formed.

Serves 6 to 8

Potatoes can be baked the day before.

Lucy Inman, Atlanta, GA

Sweet Potato Delight

Casserole
8	sweet potatoes, mashed
¼	cup butter, melted
1	cup sugar
½	cup milk
3	eggs, beaten
1	tablespoon vanilla extract

Topping
1	cup brown sugar
½	cup self-rising flour
½	cup butter
1	cup chopped nuts

To prepare casserole, mix together potatoes, melted butter, sugar, milk, eggs and vanilla. Spoon into buttered 1½ to 2 quart baking dish. To prepare topping, mix together brown sugar and flour; cut in butter. Mixture will be crumbly. Stir in nuts. Sprinkle over potato mixture and bake in preheated 350 degree oven for 20 minutes.

Freezes well.

Valerie Burdette Orr

Baked Rice

3	cups cooked rice
1	cup chopped parsley
½	cup grated Cheddar cheese
⅓	cup chopped onion
¼	cup chopped green pepper
1	garlic clove, minced
1	14½-ounce can evaporated milk
2	eggs, beaten
½	cup vegetable oil
1	tablespoon salt
½	teaspoon seasoned salt
½	teaspoon pepper
¼	teaspoon MSG (optional)
	juice of 1 lemon
	zest of 1 lemon
	paprika

Mix rice, parsley, cheese, onion, green pepper and garlic in large mixing bowl. Blend in milk, eggs, oil, salts, pepper, MSG, if using, lemon juice and lemon zest. Spoon into greased 2 quart casserole. Sprinkle top with paprika and bake in preheated 350 degree oven for 45 minutes or until knife inserted in center comes out clean.

Serves 10

Joyce Crichton, Kansas City, MO

Rice Dressing

1	cup chopped onions
½	cup chopped celery
½	cup butter
1	cup cooked long-grain rice
½	teaspoon thyme
½	teaspoon sage
1	cup chopped pimiento-stuffed olives
3	tablespoons juice from olives

Sauté onion and celery in butter until soft. Add rice, thyme, sage, olives and olive juice and mix well.

Serves 6

This dressing is great as a stuffing for fish or served along side or under fish.

Marty Wallace, Atlanta, GA

Black Beans and Rice

2	cups chicken broth
1	cup long-grain rice
1	medium onion, finely chopped
2	garlic cloves, minced
2	teaspoons olive oil
2	16-ounce cans black beans, rinsed and drained
1	cup canned crushed tomatoes
2	tablespoons red wine vinegar
¼	teaspoon cayenne pepper or to taste
3	tablespoons chopped cilantro, or to taste
	salt and pepper to taste

In saucepan, combine broth and rice and bring to boil. Reduce heat to low, cover tightly and simmer for 18 to 20 minutes or until rice is tender and liquid has been absorbed. While the rice is cooking, in large nonstick skillet, cook the onion and garlic in oil over moderate heat for 5 minutes, or until soft. Add beans, tomatoes, vinegar and cayenne and simmer for 5 minutes. Stir in cooked rice, cilantro and salt and pepper.

Serves 6

Marcia Bourne, Destin, FL

Asparagus Soufflé

1	cup asparagus tips, drained
1	cup grated Asiago cheese
4	large eggs
1	tablespoon self-rising flour
1	cup milk
	salt and pepper to taste

Blend asparagus, cheese, eggs, flour, milk, salt and pepper in food processor for 45 seconds. Pour asparagus mixture into greased 1½ quart casserole dish. Bake in preheated 400 degree oven for 30 minutes or until knife comes out clean. Serve immediately.

You may substitute broccoli or mushrooms.

Marilyn Cates, Atlanta, GA

Asparagus with Orange Glaze

½ cup fresh orange juice
   zest of 1 orange
1 tablespoon sugar
1 tablespoon minced fresh ginger
2 teaspoons soy sauce
2 pounds fresh asparagus, trimmed

Combine orange juice, zest, sugar, ginger and soy sauce in sealable plastic bag to make marinade and mix well. Add asparagus and refrigerate for 2 hours, turning occasionally. Remove asparagus from marinade and reserve marinade. Place asparagus in roasting pan in single layer and broil for 5 minutes or until tender. At the same time, heat marinade in saucepan on medium high heat, until it reduces by ½. Pour marinade over asparagus and serve immediately.

Debbie Goot, Atlanta, GA

Broccoli Casserole

2½ cups chopped frozen broccoli
   juice of 1 lemon
⅓ cup butter
½ cup chopped green onions
½ cup chopped parsley
½ cup chopped green bell pepper
1½ teaspoons Worcestershire sauce
¼ teaspoon red pepper
1 10¾-ounce can cream of mushroom soup
1 6-ounce roll garlic cheese, cut into small pieces
   breadcrumbs
   butter cut into small pieces

Cook broccoli according to directions on package, adding juice; drain. Melt butter in saucepan and sauté onion, parsley and green pepper until soft. Add Worcestershire, red pepper and soup and cook over medium heat until smooth. Add cheese and continue cooking until melted. Place cooked broccoli into casserole dish, add sauce and stir to blend. Sprinkle with breadcrumbs and butter. Bake in preheated 375 degree oven for 30 minutes.

Serves 6 to 8

You may substitute fresh broccoli for frozen broccoli.

This recipe may be made in advance.

Jan Buchanan, Louisville, KY

BAKED ASPARAGUS

1 bunch asparagus, cleaned and trimmed

2 tablespoons melted butter

salt and pepper to taste

Place asparagus in glass baking dish and drizzle with butter. Add salt and pepper; cover tightly with foil and bake in preheated 450 degree oven for 10 to 15 minutes.

Carol Thompson,
Atlanta, GA

Carrot Soufflé

1	pound carrots, peeled and chopped
3	large eggs, lightly beaten
½	cup sugar
½	cup butter or margarine, melted
3	tablespoons flour
1	teaspoon baking powder
1¼	teaspoons vanilla extract

Place carrots in medium saucepan with enough water to cover and bring to boil. Cook for 45 minutes or until very tender; drain. Process carrots in food processor or blender until smooth. Stir together carrot purée, eggs, sugar, butter, flour, baking powder and vanilla and spoon into lightly greased 1 quart baking dish. Bake in preheated 350 degree oven for 45 minute or until set.

Serves 8

Sweet and Sour Red Cabbage

¼	cup bacon drippings
¼	cup finely chopped onion
1	medium head red cabbage, shredded (about 8 cups)
2	medium cooking apples, peeled, cored and thinly sliced
1	cup water
½	cup wine vinegar
¼	cup packed brown sugar
1	teaspoon caraway seed
½	teaspoon salt
⅛	teaspoon pepper

Place bacon drippings in 5 quart Dutch oven and heat over medium heat. Add onion and cook until tender. Stir in cabbage, apples, water, vinegar, brown sugar, caraway seed, salt and pepper and bring to boil. Reduce heat to low, cover and simmer for 1½ hours or until cabbage is very tender, stirring occasionally.

Makes 5 cups

To microwave, in 3 quart microwave safe casserole, combine bacon drippings and onion and cover. Microwave on high for 2 minutes. Stir in cabbage, apples, water, vinegar, brown sugar, caraway seed, salt and pepper, using only ½ cup water and ¼ cup vinegar. Cover and microwave on high for 30 to 35 minutes or until cabbage is very tender, stirring occasionally. Let stand covered for 10 minutes before serving.

Joyce Preston, Kansas City, MO

CARROT PUFF

4 large potatoes, peeled and grated

6 carrots, peeled and grated

3 eggs, separated

1 teaspoon salt

¼ teaspoon pepper

Combine potatoes and carrots in large bowl. Beat egg yolks until thick and lemon colored. Mix egg yolks into potatoes and carrots and add salt and pepper. Beat egg whites until stiff peaks form and fold into vegetable mixture. Place vegetable mixture in greased casserole dish and bake in a preheated 350 degree oven for 30 to 40 minutes.

Serves 6

Jan Ruane, Glasgow, Scotland

Gratin of Cauliflower

2	pounds cauliflower, cut into florets
⅓	cup milk
4	tablespoons butter, melted
2	tablespoons Dijon mustard
	salt and pepper to taste
⅛	teaspoon nutmeg
½	cup grated Parmesan cheese

Place cauliflower in saucepan with salted water over high heat and bring to a boil. Cook uncovered for 10 minutes or until soft; drain. Place cauliflower, milk, butter and mustard in food processor and purée. Stir in salt, pepper and nutmeg. Place cauliflower in shallow baking dish and cover with cheese. Bake in preheated 350 degree oven for 30 minutes or until golden brown.

Mattie Lisenby, Atlanta, GA

Collard Greens with Bacon

2	bunches collard greens, stemmed
3	tablespoons vegetable oil
½	red onion, sliced
3	bacon strips, cut into ¼ inch strips
2	tablespoons cider vinegar
1	cup chicken stock
	hot pepper sauce to taste

Working in batches, stack greens and cut crosswise into 2 inch strips. Gather strips and cut into 2 inch pieces. Transfer greens into large bowl of cold water; swishing to remove grit. Repeat through several changes of water until greens are free of grit. Heat oil in very large skillet over medium high heat and add onion and bacon, cooking until onion is translucent, about 4 minutes. Add greens and cook; stirring until greens begin to wilt and are reduced in volume. Increase heat to high and add vinegar. Cook, scraping brown bits from bottom of skillet, until vinegar has evaporated, about 1 minute. Add stock, reduce heat and simmer covered until greens are tender. Add pepper sauce.

Mattie Lisenby, Atlanta, GA

Corn Pudding

2	eggs, slightly beaten
1	8.5-ounce box corn muffin mix
1	18-ounce can cream style corn
1	cup sour cream
1	18-ounce can whole kernel corn
½	cup margarine, melted
1	cup grated Swiss cheese, or more to taste

Combine eggs, muffin mix, cream style corn, sour cream, whole kernel corn and margarine and place in ungreased casserole dish. Bake in preheated 350 degree oven for 35 minutes. Top with cheese and bake an additional 10 minutes.

Judy Spaulding, Cumming, GA

Nancy Ricker, Tampa, FL

Early Summer Fresh Corn Pudding

1	cup heavy cream
3	eggs
⅓	cup milk
2	cups fresh corn
1	teaspoon salt
1	tablespoon sugar

Combine cream, eggs and milk in large bowl. Add corn, salt and sugar. Pour into shallow baking dish and bake in preheated 400 degree oven for 1 hour.

Patti Dimond, Atlanta, GA

Baked Eggplant

1	eggplant
1	tablespoon vegetable oil
½	cup grated onion
	basil and pepper to taste
1	cup tomato sauce
2	tablespoons grated Parmesan cheese
	chopped garlic to taste
	lemon juice to taste

Peel eggplant. Cut crosswise into ½ inch thick slices. Place eggplant slices onto baking sheet and brush with oil. Season with onion, basil and pepper. Bake in preheated 350 degree oven for 35 minutes, turning once. Top with tomato sauce, sprinkle with cheese, garlic and lemon juice and bake for an additional 5 minutes.

Florence Inman, Atlanta, GA

Corn Pie

1¼   cups fine saltine cracker crumbs
½   cup butter, melted
1¼   cups milk, divided
2   cups corn, fresh or frozen
½   teaspoon salt
¼   teaspoon white pepper
2   tablespoons instant minced onion
2   tablespoons flour
2   eggs, beaten
  paprika to taste

Combine cracker crumbs and butter in small bowl. Press all but ½ cup of crumb mixture into 9 inch pie pan to form crust. Reserve remaining ½ cup of crumb mixture. Mix 1 cup milk, corn, salt, pepper and onion in saucepan over high heat. Bring to a boil; reduce heat and simmer for 3 minutes. Combine flour and remaining milk, stir into corn mixture and cook until thickened, stirring frequently. Allow to cool slightly and gradually add eggs, stirring vigorously. Pour corn mixture into pie pan and sprinkle with reserved crumb mixture and paprika. Bake in preheated 400 degree oven for about 15 minutes. Cut into wedges and serve hot.

Serves 6

Carol Crichton, Atlanta, GA

Eggplant Casserole

1   large eggplant, sliced into ⅛ inch slices
1   large green pepper, finely chopped, divided
2   large onions, finely chopped, divided
2   14½-ounce cans stewed tomatoes, divided
  salt, pepper and garlic powder to taste
¼   teaspoon sugar, divided
10   ounces sliced Colby cheese, divided

To parboil eggplant: Bring 1 to 2 inches water to boil in skillet. Place eggplant slices in boiling water and cook until tender.

Parboil eggplant slices for about 10 minutes and drain onto plate covered with paper towels. In deep 8x10 inch casserole dish, layer ½ the eggplant, slightly overlapping slices, ½ the green pepper, ½ the onion, 1 can stewed tomatoes, breaking tomatoes apart for better coverage, salt, pepper, garlic powder, ⅛ teaspoon sugar and ½ the cheese. Repeat layers. Bake covered in preheated 400 degree oven for 30 minutes. Reduce oven temperature to 350 degrees, uncover and bake for an additional 30 minutes. Let stand for 10 minutes and serve.

You may want to place aluminum foil or baking sheet on rack below eggplant to catch any overflow.

Connie McClellan, Marietta, GA

Green Beans, Toasted Pecans and Blue Cheese

¼	teaspoon Dijon mustard
1	teaspoon cider vinegar
2	teaspoons finely chopped shallots
1	tablespoon olive oil, divided
½	cup pecans
	salt to taste
¾	pound green beans
¼	cup blue cheese
	pepper to taste

In large bowl, whisk together mustard, vinegar, shallot and ½ tablespoon oil to make dressing. In small heavy skillet, heat remaining oil over moderately high heat until hot but not smoking and sauté pecans with salt, stirring frequently until a shade darker, about 1 minute. Transfer pecans to paper towels to drain and cool. Coarsely chop nuts. In large saucepan, blanch beans in boiling salted water until just tender, about 3 minutes, and drain in colander. Transfer beans to bowl of ice water, stirring until just cool. Drain beans well and add to dressing. Crumble blue cheese over beans and gently toss with ½ the nuts, salt and pepper. Serve beans at room temperature topped with remaining nuts.

Serves 2

Lima-Green Bean Bake

6	tablespoons butter
2	tablespoons flour
1	teaspoon salt
¼	teaspoon pepper
	dash of cayenne pepper
¼	teaspoon Worcestershire sauce
1	cup light cream
½	cup grated Parmesan cheese
1½	cups French cut green beans
1½	cups baby lima beans

Melt butter in saucepan over medium heat. Add flour, salt, pepper, cayenne and Worcestershire to saucepan and cook for 3 minutes. Add cream and when sauce thickens, add cheese, stirring until melted. Alternate layers of beans and sauce in greased 1½ quart casserole dish and bake uncovered in a preheated 300 degree oven for 1 hour.

Marilyn Cates, Atlanta, GA

Emerald Isle Sprouts

¾   cup milk
½   8-ounce package cream cheese
1   tablespoon dry sherry
1   tablespoon chopped fresh parsley
1   tablespoon minced onion
½   teaspoon salt
¾   pound fresh Brussels sprouts or 1 10-ounce package frozen,
     cooked until crisp
¼   cup breadcrumbs

Pour milk in saucepan over low heat. Add cream cheese and cook until melted. Add sherry, parsley, onion and salt and stir until smooth. Pour ½ cheese mixture into bottom of small baking dish. Arrange sprouts over sauce and add remaining sauce. Top with breadcrumbs and bake in preheated 325 degree oven for 30 minutes.

Serves 4

Marilyn Cates, Atlanta, GA

Very Best Squash Casserole

3   pounds yellow squash, peeled and sliced
4½   tablespoons chopped onion
6   tablespoons butter, melted
3   eggs, beaten
1½   cups grated Cheddar cheese, divided
¾   cup milk
1¼   cups saltine cracker crumbs, divided
     salt and pepper to taste
4   tablespoons butter, melted

Place squash and onion in saucepan with small amount of water over medium heat and cook until very soft; drain and mash with fork or chop coarsely in food processor. Place squash and onion mixture in large bowl and mix in butter and eggs. Add ¾ cup cheese, milk, 1 cup cracker crumbs, salt and pepper. Pour mixture into 3 quart lightly greased casserole dish. Combine remaining cheese with remaining cracker crumbs and spread over squash mixture; drizzle with melted butter. Bake in preheated 325 degree oven for about 1 hour or until brown and bubbly.

Serves 8 to 10

This dish freezes well.

Kathy Johnson, Atlanta, GA

Summer Squash Casserole

1	pound yellow squash, sliced
1	thinly sliced onion
½	cup butter
½	cup mayonnaise
½	cup sliced green pepper
½	cup chopped pimiento
1	cup grated cheese
	breadcrumbs

Place squash and onion in saucepan with enough water to cover; bring to a boil and cook until just tender and drain. Mix squash and onions, butter, mayonnaise, green pepper, pimiento and cheese and spoon into greased casserole dish. Bake in preheated 350 degree oven for 25 minutes. Top with breadcrumbs and bake an additional 5 minutes.

Serves 6 to 8

Robert O. Breitling, Jr., Atlanta, GA

Fresh Tomato Tart

1	unbaked 9 inch pie crust
6-8	ripe tomatoes, chopped
	salt and black pepper to taste
½	sweet onion, chopped
2	tablespoons finely chopped fresh basil
3	cups grated Cheddar cheese
½	cup mayonnaise

Bake pie crust according to directions on package and cool. Place tomatoes in colander, add salt and drain for 45 minutes. Add pepper and onion to tomatoes and place in piecrust; add a layer of basil. In medium bowl, mix cheese with just enough mayonnaise to hold it together. Place cheese on top of tomato filling. Bake in preheated 375 degree oven for 30 to 35 minutes or until cheese topping bubbles and starts to brown.

This recipe can be served hot or cold. You may also use additional herbs such as oregano, parsley or thyme, as well as other cheeses such as mozzarella.

Pamela Penn, Atlanta, GA

Similar recipe was submitted by Carol Dew, Atlanta, GA

Tomato Pie

1	deep-dish pie shell
2-3	pounds green or red tomatoes, peeled and thinly sliced
	salt and pepper to taste
1	chopped onion
½-1	pound sliced mushrooms
1	tablespoon chopped basil
6-12	bacon strips, cooked and crumbled or
	3 ounces bottled bacon bits
1	cup grated cheese — Cheddar or mozzarella or a mixture
¾	cup mayonnaise

Fill pie shell with tomatoes and sprinkle with salt and pepper. Combine onion, mushrooms, basil and bacon and place over tomatoes. Mix cheese and mayonnaise in bowl and spread over mushroom mixture. Bake in preheated 350 degree oven for 30 to 35 minutes or until brown.

Serves 6 to 8

Carol Stevens, Atlanta, GA

Vidalia Onion and Rice Bake

5½	cups boiling water
2	cups rice
¼	cup butter or margarine
8	cups chopped Vidalia onions
1	cup shredded Swiss cheese
⅔	cup half & half
	hot pepper sauce and garlic powder to taste

Combine boiling water and rice in saucepan and mix well. Cook for 5 to 7 minutes and drain. Heat butter or margarine in skillet; add onion and sauté until tender. Remove from heat. Stir in rice, cheese, half & half, pepper sauce and garlic powder. Spoon onion mixture into greased 2 quart baking dish and bake in preheated 350 degree oven for 1 hour.

Serves 8

You may substitute Jarlsberg cheese for Cheddar.

Faye Donaldson, Atlanta, GA

Similar recipe contributed by Alana Shepherd, Atlanta, GA

Glorified Zucchini

ZUCCHINI RIBBONS

1-2 medium zucchini
2 tablespoons butter

Peel zucchini into long ribbons with potato peeler. Place zucchini ribbons in saucepan of boiling water and cook for 30 seconds. Drain water from saucepan, add butter and toss. Serve immediately.

Serves 2

Marilyn Cates, Atlanta, GA

5	medium zucchini, sliced 1 inch thick
2	tablespoons butter
1	large Vidalia onion, chopped
2	tablespoons flour
½	cup white wine
1	10¾-ounce can cream of mushroom soup
	salt to taste
	breadcrumbs
	grated cheese, preferably a mild or sharp Cheddar to taste

Place zucchini in skillet on medium low heat; cook slightly and drain. Place zucchini in greased 9x11 inch baking dish. Place butter in skillet on medium heat and melt; add onion and brown. Stir in flour, wine, soup and salt. Pour or spread onion mixture evenly over zucchini. Sprinkle with breadcrumbs and cheese. Bake in preheated 350 degree oven for 30 to 40 minutes.

Serves 6 to 8

This recipe may be doubled easily and freezes well.

Elizabeth Neal, Rome, GA

Desserts

Baked Alaska

1⅓	cups crushed shortbread cookies
½	cup finely chopped pecans
⅓	cup brown sugar
6	tablespoons butter, melted
½	cup water
10	tablespoons sugar, divided
2	tablespoons crème de menthe
1	quart vanilla ice cream, divided
½	cup whipping cream
	green food coloring
3	egg whites
⅛	teaspoon cream of tartar
3	teaspoons water

Combine cookie crumbs, pecans, brown sugar and butter in bowl. Press mixture firmly over bottom and side of 9 inch pie plate. Bake in preheated 325 degree oven for 10 minutes. Cool completely. Combine water with 4 tablespoons sugar in small saucepan; cover. Bring to boil and uncover. Continue boiling without stirring for 7 minutes. Remove from heat and cool slightly. Add crème de menthe; cool. Spread ½ of ice cream in layer on pie shell and freeze until firm. Combine whipping cream and food coloring and beat until stiff. Add 2 tablespoons crème de menthe syrup. Spread over ice cream. Freeze. Top with remaining ice cream. Freeze. Beat egg whites with cream of tartar until peaks form. Beat in remaining sugar and 3 teaspoons water. Cover ice cream with the meringue and seal well to edges. Freeze overnight. This will keep in freezer for one week. When ready to serve, place on board covered with aluminum foil and bake in preheated 450 degree oven for 4 minutes. Cut into 8 pieces and drizzle remaining crème de menthe syrup over each serving.

Serves 8

Elaine Bennett, Louisville, KY

Bibi's Lemon Ice Cream

½   cup lemon juice, freshly squeezed
1   tablespoon finely minced lemon zest
2   cups sugar
4   cups half & half
      yellow food coloring

Mix lemon juice, zest and sugar in medium bowl. Stir in half & half and food coloring. Put mixture in refrigerator until very cold. Freeze according to ice cream freezer directions.

The ice cream is tangy and creamy; it is great with fresh berries. The recipe may easily be doubled.

Kathy Johnson, Atlanta, GA

Creamy Mocha Frozen Dessert

Crust
1   cup chocolate wafer cookie crumbs
½   cup finely chopped pecans
¼   cup butter, melted

Filling
2   8-ounce packages cream cheese, softened
1   14-ounce can sweetened condensed milk
½   cup chocolate flavored syrup
2   teaspoons instant coffee
1   tablespoon hot water
1   8-ounce container frozen whipped topping, thawed
¼   cup chopped pecans

To prepare crust, combine cookie crumbs, pecans and butter in medium bowl. Blend well and press firmly into bottom of 13x9 inch pan or 10 inch pan. To prepare filling, beat cream cheese in large bowl until fluffy. Beat in condensed milk and chocolate syrup until smooth. In small bowl, combine instant coffee and water; add to cream cheese mixture. Fold in whipped topping and spoon into prepared crust. Sprinkle evenly with pecans. Freeze overnight or until firm.

Serves 15 to 16

Jean T. Gregory, San Jose, CA

CITRUS GELATO

1 14-ounce can sweetened condensed milk
⅓ cup fresh lemon juice
½ cup fresh orange juice
zest of 1 orange

Combine condensed milk and lemon juice. Add orange juice and zest. Freeze.

For variation, add ⅓ cup cream of coconut and increase orange juice to ¾ cup. This dessert is very rich so use small servings.

Maryann Busby, Atlanta, GA

Frozen Soufflé with Hot Strawberry Sauce

Soufflé
- 8 macaroons, crumbled
- 5 tablespoons orange juice or Grand Marnier
- ½ gallon vanilla ice cream, softened
- 2 cups heavy cream
- 6-8 tablespoons chopped almonds, toasted
  powdered sugar

Hot Strawberry Sauce
- 2 pints strawberries, hulled and cut in half
- ½ cup sugar
- 8 teaspoons orange juice or Grand Marnier

To prepare soufflé, stir crumbled macaroons and orange juice or Grand Marnier into ice cream. Whip cream until thick and shiny. Fold into ice cream mixture. Spoon into mold and sprinkle surface lightly with almonds and powdered sugar. Cover with plastic wrap and freeze until firm, about 5 hours, or overnight. To prepare sauce just before serving, put berries in saucepan with sugar and simmer until soft. Remove from heat and stir in orange juice or Grand Marnier. Serve sauce over frozen soufflé.

Two 10-ounce packages frozen strawberries can be substituted for fresh. Adjust sugar if frozen strawberries are used.

Serves 10 to 12

CRANBERRY CHARDONNAY SORBET

1 cup sugar
1 cup light corn syrup
2 cups Chardonnay wine
4 cups cranberry juice

Heat sugar, corn syrup and wine in saucepan until sugar is dissolved. Add cranberry juice and mix well. Let cool to room temperature. Add mixture to sorbet/ice cream maker and follow directions for freezing.

This sorbet is light, tangy and delicious.

The Swag, Waynesville, NC

Cranapple Delight

- 3 cups diced apples, unpeeled
- 2 cups fresh cranberries
- 1 cup sugar
- ½ cup butter, melted
- ½ cup chopped nuts
- ½ cup brown sugar, packed tightly
- 1½ cups uncooked rolled oats
- ⅓ cup flour

Roll apples and cranberries in sugar. Place in greased 9x12 inch baking dish. Mix butter, nuts, brown sugar, oats and flour. Sprinkle evenly over apples and cranberries. Bake in preheated 350 degree oven for 45 minutes.

Serves 12 to 14

Red Delicious apples are delicious used in this recipe.

June Weitnauer, Atlanta, GA

Beverly's Cobbler

½	cup butter
1	cup flour
1	cup sugar
1	teaspoon baking powder
1	teaspoon baking soda
½	teaspoon salt
1	cup milk
2½	cups fresh fruit

Melt butter in 8 or 9 inch baking dish. Mix flour, sugar, baking powder, soda, salt and milk in a bowl. Pour batter over butter; do not stir, just smooth out. Use any kind of fresh fruit, such as peaches, blueberries, raspberries or apples, to put over batter. Bake in preheated 350 degree oven until top is brown, about 30 minutes.

Serves 5 to 6

This fresh fruit cobbler is a recipe from one of Highlands' best caterers; it is quick and easy. It also freezes well.

For variation, instead of fresh fruit, substitute 1 29-ounce can of sliced peaches and 1 8-ounce can of crushed pineapple. Drain ½ of juice from each can before stirring fruit into batter. Bake as above.

Martha Lou Riddle, Rome, GA

Similar recipe submitted by Linda Putnam, Fayetteville, GA

Moroccan Orange Salad

6	naval or temple oranges
1½	teaspoons rose water or orange water
2	tablespoons powdered sugar
¼	teaspoon cinnamon

Peel, seed and slice the oranges into very thin slices. Arrange in overlapping circles in serving dish. Sprinkle with rose water or orange water, sugar and cinnamon. Taste for sweetness and adjust as needed. Chill until ready to serve and dust with more cinnamon.

Orange water and rose water can be found at ethnic grocery stores in Atlanta.

Robert O. Breitling, Jr., Atlanta, GA

Banana Pudding

2	cups half & half
1	cup milk
1	5.1-ounce package vanilla instant pudding mix
1	12-ounce package vanilla wafers
6	bananas
4	egg whites
⅓	cup sugar
½	teaspoon vanilla extract

Combine half & half, milk and pudding mix in large bowl. Beat at low speed until blended. Beat at medium speed 2 minutes or until mixture is smooth and thickened. Layer ¼ of wafers in 2½ quart baking dish. Slice 2 bananas and layer over wafers. Pour ⅓ pudding over bananas. Repeat layers twice, ending with pudding. Arrange remaining wafers around edge of baking dish. To prepare meringue, beat egg whites at high speed until foamy. Add sugar, 1 tablespoon at a time, beating 2 to 4 minutes until peaks form and sugar dissolves. Fold in vanilla. Spread meringue over pudding, sealing to edge of dish. Bake in preheated 325 degree oven for 20 minutes or until golden.

Serves 8

Susan Taulman, Atlanta, GA

Crème Brûlée

4	cups heavy cream
2	teaspoons vanilla extract
9	large egg yolks
1	cup plus 2 tablespoons sugar
⅛	teaspoon salt
¼	cup plus 2 tablespoons brown sugar, firmly packed

In saucepan, heat cream until hot but not scalded. Add vanilla and set aside. Beat egg yolks and sugar in large bowl. Add cream and salt. Divide mixture among 15 ramekins. Put into water bath. Bake in preheated 350 degree oven for 40 minutes. Let cool; refrigerate 1 hour or more. Two hours before serving, preheat broiler. Put ramekins on baking sheet. Sift brown sugar on top. Broil 6 inches from heat until sugar caramelizes, 1 or 2 minutes. Refrigerate at least 1 hour before serving.

Serves 15

Maggie Young, Atlanta, GA

Buttermilk Bread Pudding with Whiskey Sauce

Bread Pudding

¼	cup butter
1	16-ounce loaf day old French bread
4	cups buttermilk
1	cup raisins
2	eggs, lightly beaten
1⅓	cups dark brown sugar, packed
1	tablespoon vanilla extract
1½	cups plain yogurt (optional)

Whiskey Sauce

1	cup butter, softened
2	cups sugar
2	eggs, beaten
½	cup 90 proof whiskey

Preheat oven to 350 degrees. To prepare pudding, melt butter in 13x9 inch baking dish. Combine bread, buttermilk and raisins in large bowl. Set aside. Combine eggs, brown sugar, vanilla and yogurt, if using; stir well. Add egg mixture to bread mixture and stir gently. Pour into pan of melted butter and bake for 1 hour. To prepare sauce, cream butter and sugar until light and fluffy. Place in top of double boiler over boiling water. Cook about 30 minutes, stirring often until very hot. Stir small amount of hot mixture into eggs, then stir eggs into rest of hot mixture. Cook about 3 minutes more, stirring constantly. Let cool; add whiskey. If mixture seems grainy, add 2 tablespoons water.

Cherri Penton, Baton Rouge, LA

Blueberry Bread Pudding and Whiskey Sauce

Bread Pudding
1	pound 3 day old French bread
4	cups milk
6	eggs
2	cups sugar
1½	tablespoons vanilla extract
1-1½	pints fresh blueberries
	cinnamon

Whiskey Sauce
2	cups butter
2	cups sugar
3	eggs
½	cup whiskey

To prepare pudding, cut and cube French bread in large bowl and add milk, eggs, sugar, vanilla and blueberries. Mix well. Pour into lightly buttered 8x10 inch pan. Sprinkle cinnamon over top. Bake at 350 degrees for 35 to 45 minutes. To prepare sauce, heat butter and sugar in double boiler until sugar is dissolved, stirring constantly, about 15 minutes. Beat eggs in another bowl. Gradually spoon 5 tablespoons of heated butter/sugar mixture into eggs and whisk vigorously or eggs will curdle. Pour egg mixture into double boiler and stir until well mixed. Add whiskey and stir. Serve warm sauce over bread pudding.

Another fruit of choice may be substituted.

Chef Marty Rosenfield, Lakeside Restaurant, Highlands, NC

VANILLA SAUCE

2 cups whipping cream
½ cup plus
6 tablespoons sugar
2⅓ tablespoons
vanilla extract
4 tablespoons cornstarch
4 tablespoons water
¼ teaspoon salt
1 1/ tablespoons bourbon or
other liqueur
depending on use

Heat whipping cream, sugar and vanilla in saucepan. Soften cornstarch in water; when soft add to whipping cream mixture and stir slowly over low heat until thickened. Add salt and stir in bourbon to taste.

*This sauce is delicious
on bread pudding
and freezes well.*

Mary Hataway, Soiree Catering
and Events, Atlanta, GA

Gingerbread Pumpkin Trifle

2	14-ounce packages gingerbread mix
1	5.1-ounce box French vanilla pudding mix (not instant)
1	30-ounce can pumpkin pie filling
½	cup brown sugar, packed
½	teaspoon cinnamon
1	12-ounce container frozen whipped topping
⅔	cup gingersnaps, crushed.

Bake gingerbread according to directions; cool. Prepare pudding mix and let it cool. Stir pumpkin pie filling, brown sugar and cinnamon into pudding. Crumble ½ gingerbread into large attractive bowl or trifle dish. Pour ½ pudding mixture over gingerbread; add layer of ½ whipped topping. Repeat with remaining gingerbread, pudding and whipped topping. Sprinkle top with crushed gingersnaps. Refrigerate.

Serves 20

This recipe can be split into two trifles. Otherwise, you may need to use one punch bowl. It is wonderful at Thanksgiving or any other time of the year.

Jeannine Freer, Ball Ground, GA

Heavenly Chocolate Mocha Trifle

1	devil's food cake mix
2	3½-ounce packages instant chocolate pudding
½	cup coffee-flavored liqueur, divided
2	6-ounce packages bits of brickle
2	10-ounce containers frozen nondairy whipped topping
	shaved chocolate

Bake cake according to directions; cool and cut into bite size pieces. Prepare pudding according to directions. Place ½ cake pieces in large bowl; sprinkle with ¼ cup coffee-flavored liqueur. Then layer ½ prepared pudding, 1 package brickle and 1 container whipped topping. Repeat layers with remaining ingredients, starting with remaining cake pieces. Sprinkle top with shaved chocolate. Chill.

This dessert is best made ahead and chilled for one day.

Chopped English toffee can be substituted for the bits of brickle.

Dianne McKnight, Atlanta, GA

Chocolate Mousse

1   8-ounce package bittersweet chocolate, broken into pieces
1   cup light cream
4   egg yolks
    dash of salt
1   teaspoon vanilla extract
1   teaspoon instant coffee
1   cup heavy cream

Put chocolate pieces in blender. Bring light cream to boil and pour over chocolate. Blend 10 seconds. Add egg yolks and blend 5 seconds. Add salt, vanilla and coffee. Add cream and blend 10 seconds. Refrigerate for 24 hours or overnight. Pour into sherbet cups.

Serves 5 to 6

This mousse is very rich but delicious and so easy.

Eleanor Bernhardt, Atlanta, GA

White Chocolate Mousse with Raspberry Sauce

Mousse
½   pound white chocolate
1   cup heavy cream
½   cup sugar
½   cup water
3   egg whites

Raspberry Sauce
1   10-ounce package frozen raspberries
1   tablespoon Kirsch
¼   cup powdered sugar

To prepare mousse, chop chocolate fine and set aside. Whip cream; refrigerate until ready to use. Bring sugar and water to boil; cook for a few minutes to form syrup. Place egg whites in mixing bowl and beat until fairly stiff. With mixer on low, pour hot syrup slowly into egg whites. Continue to beat at low speed a few minutes longer. Fold chocolate into egg whites. Fold in whipped cream. Pour into 6 cup mold and refrigerate. To prepare sauce, defrost berries, purée and strain to remove seeds. Mix in Kirsch and sugar. More sugar may be added to taste. Chill. Pour over mousse before serving.

Serves 6 to 8

COFFEE MOUSSE

24 large marshmallows
1 cup hot strong coffee
½ cup whipping cream

Melt marshmallows in hot coffee; cool. Beat whipping cream until very stiff. Fold into marshmallow mixture and chill.

This mousse is very good and very easy to make. Use really strong coffee to get best results. Flavored coffee could be used for variety.

Eleanor Bernhardt, Atlanta, GA

Edinburgh Mist

1	cup whipping cream
1	teaspoon vanilla extract
1	tablespoon sherry or brandy
2	tablespoons sugar
1½-2	cups macaroon crumbs
¼	cup chopped almonds, toasted

Whip cream with vanilla, sherry and sugar. Gently fold in macaroon crumbs. Spoon into stem glasses and sprinkle with almonds. Chill.

Serves 6 to 8

Jan Ruane, Glasgow, Scotland

Chocolate Pecan Pie

Crust
1	cup flour
6	tablespoons unsalted butter, chilled, cut into ½ inch pieces
1	tablespoon sugar
½	teaspoon salt
2	tablespoons, plus more if needed, ice water

Filling
4	ounces bittersweet or semisweet chocolate, chopped
2	tablespoons unsalted butter
½	cup packed dark brown sugar
3	large eggs
¼	teaspoon salt
¾	cup light corn syrup
1½	cups pecan pieces, lightly toasted

To prepare crust, combine flour, butter, sugar and salt in food processor; pulse until mixture resembles coarse crumbs. Drizzle 2 tablespoons water over mixture; pulse just until moist clumps form, adding more water by teaspoonfuls if mixture is dry. Gather dough into ball and flatten into disk. Wrap dough in plastic and refrigerate for 30 minutes. (Can be prepared 1 day ahead and kept refrigerated.) Roll out dough on floured surface to 13 inch round. Transfer to 9 inch glass pie dish. Trim overhang to 1 inch; fold under and crimp decoratively and set aside. To prepare filling, stir chocolate and butter in small heavy saucepan over low heat until melted. Cool slightly. Whisk brown sugar, eggs and salt in large bowl to blend. Whisk in corn syrup and chocolate mixture. Sprinkle pecans over crust. Pour filling over pecans. Bake in preheated 325 degree oven until crust is golden and filling is puffed, about 55 minutes. Cool pie completely on wire rack.

Serves 6 to 8

Kevin C. Sharkey, Charlotte, NC

Lemon Meringue Fluff

     4   eggs, separated
     1   teaspoon cream of tartar
     1½ cups sugar, divided
     3   tablespoons lemon juice
     3   teaspoons lemon rind
     1   cup whipping cream
     ½   cup coconut flakes, toasted (optional)

Lightly grease 8x12 inch pan. Beat 4 egg whites until peaks form; add cream of tartar and gradually add 1 cup sugar while beating. Beat until stiff and entire cup sugar is incorporated. Spread evenly in prepared pan and bake in 275 degree oven for 55 minutes. Cool. Beat egg yolks; add remaining sugar, lemon juice and lemon rind. Pour into saucepan and cook, stirring until custard thickens. Cool. When meringue and custard have cooled, whip cream until stiff. Spread thin layer of cream over baked meringue; spread lemon custard over cream and top with remaining cream. Sprinkle with toasted coconut. Refrigerate overnight.

Serves 12

Jean T. Gregory, San Jose, CA

Favorite Chocolate Pie

     1½ cups sugar
     3   tablespoons cocoa powder
     ¼   cup melted butter
     2   eggs
         dash of salt
     1   5-ounce can evaporated milk
     1   teaspoon vanilla extract
     1   uncooked pie crust
     2   cups heavy whipping cream

Combine sugar, cocoa powder and butter in mixing bowl. Add eggs and beat with mixer for 2½ minutes. Add salt, milk and vanilla and beat until mixed. Pour into pie crust and bake in preheated 350 degree oven for 35 to 45 minutes. Cool on wire rack for 30 minutes; refrigerate until completely cool. Whip the cream and cover entire pie.

Elspeth Willcoxon, Atlanta, GA

Coconut Key Lime Pie

6	eggs
2	14-ounce cans sweetened condensed milk
	zest of 2 limes
	juice of 2 limes
	Key lime juice
1	cup sweetened coconut, toasted
2	graham crust pie shells

In large bowl, beat eggs; add milk and zest. Pour lime juice into measuring cup and add enough key lime juice to measure 1 cup. Stir juice into egg and milk mixture. Divide coconut equally into bottom of each pie shell. Pour mixture equally into shells and bake in preheated 350 degree oven for 15 to 20 minutes, or until center is set.

Constance L. Preston, Savannah, GA

Tantalizing Tiramisu Toffee Pie

1½	tablespoons instant coffee granules
¾	cup warm water
1	10 to 12-ounce fresh or frozen (thawed) pound cake
1	8-ounce package cream cheese, softened
½	cup chocolate syrup
½	cup powdered sugar
½	teaspoon cinnamon
1	16-ounce container frozen whipped topping, thawed and divided
2	1½-ounce English toffee candy bars, chopped coarsely

Stir together coffee and warm water until coffee is dissolved. Place in refrigerator to cool. Cut cake into approximately 14 slices and cut each slice in half diagonally. Place cake triangles in bottom and up side of an attractive bowl or deep-dish pie plate. Drizzle cooled coffee over the cake. Beat cream cheese, chocolate syrup, sugar, and cinnamon with electric mixer at medium speed until smooth. Add ½ whipped topping, beating until fluffy. Spread cream cheese mixture evenly over cake. Spoon remaining whipped topping around edges and sprinkle pie with candy. Chill 8 hours or overnight.

Coffee liqueur may be substituted for instant coffee, and low fat cream cheese and whipped topping can be used.

Bobbie Kirkland, Ball Ground, GA

COCONUT FUDGE PIE

1 cup butter

1 6-ounce package semisweet chocolate chips

4 eggs

1 cup chopped pecans

1 cup coconut

2 cups sugar

1 teaspoon vanilla extract

2 deep-dish pie shells

Melt together butter and chocolate chips; stir until smooth. Add eggs, pecans, coconut, sugar and vanilla and stir until well mixed. Pour into pie shells and bake in preheated 350 degree oven for 45 minutes.

Dianne McKnight, Alpharetta, GA

Cranberry Pie

1	frozen pie crust
1	8-ounce package cream cheese, softened
¼	cup sugar
1	8-ounce container frozen nondairy whipped topping
1	16-ounce can whole berry cranberry sauce
½	teaspoon vanilla extract

Bake pie crust according to package directions. Beat cream cheese and sugar until well mixed; add whipped topping and beat until smooth. Stir in cranberry sauce and vanilla. Spoon into pie crust. Freeze at least 4 hours. Remove from freezer 15 minutes before serving.

Martha Lou Riddle, Rome, GA

Sour Cream Apple Pie

Pie

2¼	cups sugar
6	tablespoons flour
1½	teaspoons salt
3	cups sour cream
3	teaspoons vanilla extract
3	eggs
6	cups finely sliced apples
2	9-inch unbaked pie shells

Topping

⅔	cup sugar
⅔	cup flour
2	teaspoons cinnamon
½	cup butter
1½	cups chopped walnuts

To prepare pie, mix together sugar, flour and salt; mix and add sour cream, vanilla, eggs and apples. Pour into pie shells and bake in preheated 425 degree oven for 15 minutes. Lower temperature to 350 degrees; bake for 30 minutes. Remove pie from oven. To prepare topping, combine sugar, flour and cinnamon; cut in butter. Add walnuts and sprinkle over pies. Return pies to oven and bake for 15 minutes.

Makes 2 pies

Lemonade Stand Pie

1	6-ounce can pink lemonade concentrate, partially thawed
1	pint vanilla ice cream, softened
1	8-ounce container nondairy whipped topping, thawed
1	graham cracker crust
	strawberries for garnish

In large bowl, beat lemonade concentrate for 30 seconds at low speed with electric mixer. Gradually spoon in softened ice cream; beat until blended. Fold in whipped topping and spoon into crust. Freeze 4 hours or overnight. Let stand 15 to 20 minutes before cutting. Garnish with strawberries.

Marilyn Cates, Atlanta, GA

Walnut Pie

3	large eggs, slightly beaten
1	cup dark corn syrup
¾	cup sugar
2	tablespoons melted butter
1	teaspoon vanilla extract
½	teaspoon salt
¼	cup brandy (optional)
1¼	cups chopped walnuts
1	9-inch frozen unbaked pie shell

Place baking sheet on oven rack and preheat oven to 350 degrees. In medium mixing bowl, mix together eggs, corn syrup, sugar, butter, vanilla, salt and brandy. Sir in nuts and pour into pie shell. Place on baking sheet and bake 50 to 55 minutes or until crust is golden brown. Remove from oven and allow to cool on wire rack.

Serve warm with whipped cream or à la mode.

Bart Marks, Atlanta, GA

Aunt Lena's Chocolate Chip Cookies

If brown sugar has become rock hard, use grater to provide the amount you need.

2	cups flour
1	teaspoon baking soda
½	teaspoon salt
¾	cup butter
1	cup firmly packed brown sugar
¼	cup sugar
1	egg, unbeaten
2	teaspoons vanilla extract
1	12-ounce package semisweet chocolate chips

Sift together flour, soda and salt; set aside. Cream butter; add sugars and mix until creamy. Add egg and vanilla. Gradually mix in dry ingredients. Stir in chips. Drop by rounded teaspoonfuls on ungreased baking sheets. Bake in preheated 325 degree oven for 10 to 11 minutes.

Makes 5 dozen

Cookie Aftergut, Atlanta, GA

Betsy's Cookies

½	cup butter
½	cup chunky peanut butter
1¼	cups flour, divided
½	teaspoon salt
½	teaspoon baking soda
½	teaspoon baking powder
½	cup brown sugar
½	cup sugar plus more for rolling
1	teaspoon vanilla extract
1	egg
2	cups butterscotch chips
2	cups semisweet chocolate chips

Beat together butter and peanut butter until creamy. Add ½ cup flour, salt, soda, baking powder, sugars, vanilla and egg; mix well. Add remaining flour and mix well. Stir in butterscotch and chocolate chips. Form into 2 inch balls, roll in sugar and place on ungreased baking sheets. Bake in preheated 350 degree oven for 12 to 15 minutes.

Makes 2 dozen

Betsy Fox, Lilburn, GA

Chocolate Chewies

3	cups powdered sugar
⅔	cup cocoa powder
1	teaspoon powdered, not granules, instant coffee
2	tablespoons flour
	pinch of salt
3	egg whites
½	teaspoon vanilla extract
2	cups pecans, finely chopped

Place sugar, cocoa powder, coffee, flour, salt, egg whites and vanilla in small bowl. Mix at low speed until ingredients are combined and then at high speed for 1 minute. Stir in nuts. Drop by tablespoonfuls, 1 inch apart, on baking sheets lined with parchment paper or aluminum foil, shiny side up. Bake in preheated 350 degree oven for 15 minutes, reversing sheets once during baking to ensure even baking. When done, the cookies should be dry, crisp and shiny on the outside and wet and chewy on the inside. Remove from pans and cool. Store in airtight container.

Janet Sunshine, Atlanta, GA

Chocolate Meltaways

1	cup butter
1	cup vegetable oil
1	cup sugar plus additional for rolling
1	cup powdered sugar
2	eggs
1	teaspoon vanilla extract
4	cups flour
1	teaspoon baking soda
1	teaspoon cream of tartar
1	teaspoon salt
1	12-ounce package chocolate chips

Combine butter, oil, sugars, eggs and vanilla. Beat until smooth and well blended. Add flour, soda, cream of tartar and salt. Mix until well combined. Stir in chocolate chips. Shape into 1 inch balls and roll in sugar. Place 2 inches apart on ungreased baking sheet. Bake in preheated 350 degree oven for 10 to 12 minutes.

Carol Sharkey, Atlanta, GA

Chocolate Fudge Meringues

Chocolate Fudge Filling
1	6-ounce package semisweet chocolate chips
3	tablespoons butter
4	egg yolks, slightly beaten
2	tablespoons corn syrup

Meringues
4	egg whites
¼	teaspoon cream of tartar
½	teaspoon salt
1	cup sugar
½	teaspoon almond extract
½	teaspoon vanilla extract
	chopped Brazil nuts for topping

To prepare filling, melt chocolate chips with butter in top part of double boiler. Add egg yolks and corn syrup. Cook, stirring, for 5 minutes. Remove from heat. Beat until mixture cools to spreading consistency. To prepare meringues, beat egg whites until foamy. Add cream of tartar and salt and beat until whites begin to hold their shape. Gradually add sugar, beating until stiff but not dry. Add extracts. Drop by teaspoonfuls onto baking sheet covered with heavy wax paper. With a teaspoon, make a depression in center of each and fill with Chocolate Fudge mixture. Sprinkle with nuts. Bake in preheated 300 degree oven for 25 minutes.

Carol Sharkey, Atlanta, GA

Do not use salted butter to grease the pan for cookies. This practice could cause sticking or the cookies to get too brown on the bottom. Using parchment paper instead produces more evenly browned cookies.

Cornflakes Cereal Cookies

1	scant cup sugar
1	cup butter or margarine
1	teaspoon baking soda
1	teaspoon cream of tartar
1	teaspoon vanilla extract
1½	cups flour
2	cups cornflakes cereal, crushed

Mix together sugar, butter or margarine, soda, cream of tartar, vanilla and flour; stir in cereal. Drop by teaspoonfuls on ungreased baking sheet and bake in preheated 350 degree oven for 12 minutes. Cool on wire rack. Cookies should be very crisp after they have been out of oven for a few minutes.

Sharon Tatom, Tucson, AZ

Crunchy Chocolate Chip Cookies

Always preheat oven before baking cookies. Position cookie rack at highest level and do not open oven door during cooking. Use timer instead. Opening door will cause a drop in temperature and affect the outcome.

1	cup brown sugar
1	cup sugar
1	cup margarine
1	cup vegetable oil
1	egg
2	teaspoons vanilla extract
3½	cups flour
1	teaspoon salt
1	teaspoon cream of tartar
1	teaspoon baking soda
2	cup rolled oats
1	cup crisp rice cereal
1	cup coconut
1	cup semisweet chocolate chips

Cream together sugars and margarine; add oil, egg and vanilla and mix until blended. Stir together flour, salt, cream of tartar and soda; gradually add to butter mixture and mix until combined. Stir in oats, cereal, coconut and chocolate chips. Drop by teaspoonfuls on ungreased baking sheet and bake in preheated 350 degree oven for 12 to 15 minutes.

Erna Spears, Kansas City, MO

Ginny's Favorite Cookies

1	cup butter
1	cup brown sugar
1	egg yolk, slightly beaten
1	teaspoon vanilla extract
2	cups flour, sifted
12	ounces milk chocolate
1	cup chopped nuts

Cream together butter and sugar; add egg and vanilla. Add flour and stir until well combined. Spread thinly on jelly-roll pan and bake in preheated 350 degree oven for 15 to 20 minutes. While still warm, melt chocolate and spread over cookie; sprinkle with nuts. Cut into squares.

Hortense Wolf, Atlanta, GA

Fruit and Nut Jumbles

1¼	cups flour
¾	teaspoon baking soda
½	teaspoon cinnamon
⅛	teaspoon salt
1	cup semisweet chocolate chips
¾	cup chopped walnuts
¾	cup chopped pecans
¾	cup unblanched chopped almonds
1	cup dried cranberries
¼	cup dried sour cherries
½	cup dried blueberries
½	cup unsalted butter, softened
¾	cup sugar
¼	cup packed light brown sugar
1	egg
1	teaspoon vanilla extract

When rolling out cookie dough to cut, use a thin dusting of powdered sugar instead of flour on the board. Flour can make the dough heavier and thicker while the sugar will help the cookies brown evenly.

In a medium bowl, sift together flour, soda, cinnamon and salt. In a large bowl, mix the chocolate chips, walnuts, pecans, almonds, dried cranberries, cherries and blueberries. In another large bowl, using electric mixer, beat butter for about 1 minute, until creamy. Add sugars and beat for 1 to 2 minutes, until light and fluffy. Beat in egg and vanilla. On low speed, beat in flour mixture until blended, then stir in nuts and dried fruits until combined. Drop by rounded tablespoonfuls, 2 inches apart, on two large, ungreased baking sheets. Bake in preheated 375 degree oven for 12 to 15 minutes, until golden brown, rotating baking sheets between top and bottom shelves and from front to back halfway through cooking time. Remove baking sheets from oven and place on wire racks; cool slightly. Move cookies to wire racks and cool completely. Repeat with remaining dough. Store in airtight containers.

Makes 3 dozen

If dough seems soft, refrigerate for 15 minutes before dropping onto the baking sheets. This keeps the batter from spreading too much.

Debbie Goot, Atlanta, GA

Luscious Lemon Squares

First Layer
½   cup butter
1   cup flour, sifted
¼   cup powdered sugar

Second Layer
2   tablespoons lemon juice
    zest of 1 lemon
2   eggs, well beaten
1   cup sugar
2   tablespoons flour
½   teaspoon baking powder

Third Layer
¾   cup powdered sugar
1   teaspoon vanilla extract
1   tablespoon butter
1   tablespoon milk
1   cup shredded coconut

To prepare the first layer, mix butter with flour and add powdered sugar. Press mixture into bottom of 9 inch square pan. Bake in preheated 350 degree oven for 15 minutes; cool for 15 minutes. To prepare second layer, blend lemon juice, lemon zest, eggs, sugar, flour and baking powder. Pour over baked layer and bake for 25 minutes. To prepare third layer, blend together powdered sugar, vanilla, butter, milk and coconut and spread over filling. Cut into small squares and serve.

Jackie Fryer, Atlanta, GA

Pecan Blondies

½   cup butter, melted
1   16-ounce box light brown sugar
3   eggs
2   cups self-rising flour
1   teaspoon vanilla extract
2   cups chopped pecans

Combine butter and sugar; add eggs one at a time, beating well after each addition. Blend in flour and vanilla. Add pecans and mix well. Pour into greased and floured 9x13 inch pan and bake in preheated 325 degree oven for 45 minutes or until brown.

Mary Ann Sikes, Atlanta, GA

Mocha-Almond Biscotti

½   cup butter or margarine, melted
1   cup sugar
2   large eggs
1½ tablespoons coffee liqueur
2¼ cups flour
1½ teaspoons baking powder
¼   teaspoon salt
1½ tablespoons cocoa powder
1   cup whole almonds

To keep dough from sticking to the cutter, chill dough thoroughly. Spray cutter with a nonstick spray frequently.

Combine butter and sugar in a large bowl; beat at medium speed with electric mixer until light and fluffy. Add eggs, beating well. Mix in liqueur. Combine flour, baking powder, salt and cocoa powder; add to butter mixture, beating well to combine. Stir in almonds. Divide dough in half; shape each portion into 9x2 inch log on a greased baking sheet. Bake in preheated 350 degree oven for 30 minutes or until firm. Cool on baking sheet 5 minutes. Remove to wire racks and cool completely. Cut each log diagonally into ½ inch thick slices with serrated knife, using a gentle sawing motion. Place on ungreased baking sheets. Bake at 350 degrees for 5 to 7 minutes. Turn cookies over and bake 5 to 7 additional minutes. Remove to wire racks.

Makes 2½ dozen

1½ tablespoons chocolate syrup may be substituted for coffee liqueur
Susan Taulman, Atlanta, GA

Peanut Butter Cookies

1   cup peanut butter, creamy or chunky
1   cup sugar
1   large egg
1   teaspoon baking soda

In a bowl with an electric mixer, beat together peanut butter and sugar until well combined. In a small bowl, lightly beat egg and beat into peanut butter mixture with soda until well combined. Roll level teaspoonfuls of dough into balls and arrange about 1 inch apart on greased baking sheets. With tines of a fork, flatten balls to about 1½ inches in diameter, making a crosshatch pattern. Bake cookies in batches in middle of preheated 350 degree oven until puffed and pale golden, about 10 minutes. Cool on baking sheets for 2 minutes and transfer with a metal spatula to racks to cool completely.

Makes 6 dozen

Cookies may be kept in an airtight container at room temperature for 5 days.

Coconut Macaroons

When baking crispy cookie bars, cut while still warm to prevent crumbling.

5⅓   cups coconut flakes
1   14-ounce can sweetened condensed milk
2   teaspoons vanilla extract

Mix together coconut, condensed milk and vanilla in large bowl. Drop by teaspoonfuls on greased cookie sheet, 1 inch apart. Bake in preheated 350 degree oven for 10 to12 minutes or until golden brown. Remove from pan and cool on wire racks.

Maggie Young, Atlanta, GA

Outrageous Brownies

2   cups unsalted butter
5   cups semisweet chocolate chips, divided
6   ounces bittersweet chocolate
6   extra large eggs
3   tablespoons instant coffee granules
2   tablespoons vanilla extract
2¼   cups sugar
1¼   cups flour, divided
1   tablespoon baking powder
1   teaspoon salt
3   cups chopped walnuts

Melt together butter, 3 cups chocolate chips and bittersweet chocolate in a medium bowl over simmering water (similar to a double boiler). Allow to cool slightly. In a large bowl, stir, but do not beat, together eggs, coffee granules, vanilla and sugar. Stir the warm chocolate mixture into the egg mixture and allow to cool to room temperature. In a medium bowl, sift together 1 cup flour, baking powder and salt. Add to cooled chocolate mixture. Toss the walnuts and remaining chocolate chips in a medium bowl with the remaining ¼ cup flour; add to chocolate batter. Pour into a greased and floured 12x18x1 inch baking sheet. Bake in preheated 350 degree oven for 20 minutes, then rap the baking sheet against the oven shelf to force the air to escape from between the pan and the brownie dough. Bake for an additional 15 minutes or until a toothpick inserted in center comes out clean. Do not over bake. Allow to cool thoroughly; refrigerate and cut into large squares.

Marian Taulman Bales, Gallatin Gateway, MT

Pumpkin Squares

First Layer

1	18¼-ounce box yellow cake mix
½	cup margarine, melted
2	tablespoons water
1	egg

Second Layer

1	30-ounce can pumpkin
3	eggs
¾	cup sugar
1	14-ounce can sweetened condensed milk

Third Layer

1	cup dry yellow cake mix
2	tablespoons melted margarine
¼	cup sugar
1	teaspoon cinnamon
1	cup chopped nuts

To prepare first layer, mix together cake mix, reserving 1 cup for third layer, margarine, water and egg. Press into a greased 9x13 inch pan and bake in preheated 350 degree oven for 10 to 15 minutes, until center is firm; cool. To prepare the second layer, mix together pumpkin, eggs, sugar and milk and pour over cooled cake. To prepare third layer, mix together reserved cake mix, margarine, sugar, cinnamon and nuts. Spread over top and bake for 50 to 60 minutes. Cool and cut into squares.

Hope Harrison, Atlanta, GA

Do not substitute whipped or diet margarine when baking cookie bars. They will not cook properly or have the right texture.

Almond Crusted Cheese Cake

*Replacing sugar with
granulated sugar
substitutes in baking:*

*Most recipes require some
sugar for proper volume,
texture and browning.
The leading manufacturers
of granular sugar
substitutes suggest replacing
half the sugar with an
equivalent amount of
granular sugar substitute.*

*¼ cup sugar = 6 packets
or 2 teaspoons bulk*

*⅓ cup sugar = 8 packets or
2½ teaspoons bulk*

*½ cup sugar = 12 packets
or 4 teaspoons bulk*

*1 cup sugar = 24 packets
or 8 teaspoons bulk*

Crust

1½	cups graham cracker crumbs
4	tablespoons ground unblanched almonds
6	tablespoons sugar
¼	cup coffee cream
½	cup melted butter

Filling

4	eggs
1	cup plus 2 tablespoons sugar, divided
1½	tablespoons brandy
3	8-ounce packages cream cheese
2	cups sour cream

Sauce

2	cups fresh or frozen blueberries
⅔	cup sugar
½	cup water
1	tablespoon lemon juice
1	teaspoon cornstarch
⅓	cup water

To prepare crust, mix together graham cracker crumbs, almonds, sugar, coffee cream and melted butter and press into bottom of 10 inch springform pan. To prepare filling, beat eggs, 1 cup sugar, brandy and cheese together for 20 minutes with electric mixer. Pour over crust in pan and bake in preheated 350 degree oven for 30 minutes. Cool for 15 minutes. Mix sour cream with remaining sugar; spread over cake and return to oven. Bake 10 minutes. To prepare sauce, heat blueberries with sugar, ½ cup water and lemon juice. Combine cornstarch and ⅓ cup water; add to blueberries and cook until thickened. Refrigerate for at least 12 hours before cutting and serving.

Apricot Spice Cake

Cake
2	cups self-rising flour
1¾	cups sugar
1¼	cups chopped pecans
1	cup vegetable oil
1	6-ounce jar apricot baby food
1	teaspoon ground cinnamon
1	teaspoon ground allspice
3	eggs, lightly beaten

Cream Cheese Glaze
1	3-ounce package cream cheese, softened
3	tablespoons milk
1	teaspoon vanilla extract
	dash of salt
1½	cups sifted powdered sugar

To prepare cake, combine flour, sugar, pecans, oil, baby food, cinnamon, allspice and eggs in large bowl; stir until blended. Pour batter into heavily greased and floured 12 cup Bundt pan; batter will be shallow in pan. Bake in preheated 350 degree oven for 50 minutes or until wooden pick inserted in center comes out clean. Cool in pan on wire rack for 10 minutes. Remove from pan and cool completely on wire rack. To prepare glaze, combine cream cheese, milk, vanilla and salt; beat at medium speed with electric mixer until smooth. Gradually add powdered sugar, beating at low speed until glaze is smooth. Drizzle glaze over cake.

Do not substitute a tube pan in this recipe as the cake will be too shallow.

Susan Taulman, Atlanta, GA

Chocolate Chip Cake

1	18¼-ounce box chocolate cake mix
1	3.9-ounce box chocolate instant pudding
4	eggs
½	cup vegetable oil
1	cup sour cream
1	12-ounce package milk chocolate chips

Blend together cake mix, pudding, eggs, oil and sour cream. Stir in chocolate chips. Pour into greased and floured Bundt pan. Bake in preheated 350 degree oven for 55 to 60 minutes or until cake springs back when touched.

Cake may be topped with your favorite frosting or dusted with powdered sugar.

Jane Apple, Atlanta, GA

Butter Rum Cake

Cake
¾	cup chopped pecans
1	18¼-ounce box yellow cake mix
1	3.9-ounce box instant French vanilla pudding
½	cup vegetable oil
½	cup water
½	cup light dry rum
4	eggs

Glaze
1	cup sugar
½	cup butter
¼	cup light dry rum
¼	cup water

To prepare cake, grease and flour a tube or Bundt pan. Line the bottom of pan with chopped pecans. In large bowl, mix together cake mix and pudding; add oil, water and rum and beat well. Add eggs, one at a time, beating well after each addition. Although mixture should be smooth, do not mix too long. Pour batter into prepared pan and bake in preheated 325 degree oven for 1 hour. Begin to prepare glaze 15 minutes before cake is done. Combine sugar, butter, rum and water in small saucepan and boil gently for about 1 minute. When cake tests done with toothpick, remove from oven and poke holes all over and pour glaze over holes, reserving 1/4 cup. Let cake sit in pan, with glaze added, for 20 minutes; remove from pan, turning it onto serving plate and drizzle with remaining glaze.

Serves 12

Peggy Slotin, Atlanta, GA

Chocolate Toffee Bar Cookies

56   saltine crackers
1   cup butter
1   cup brown sugar
¼   teaspoon baking soda
2   cups chocolate chips
1   cup chopped pecans

Line large baking sheet with foil and coat with vegetable cooking spray. Lay crackers to cover baking sheet. In small saucepan, melt butter over medium heat; add brown sugar and bring to boil. Boil for 1 minute only. Remove from heat and add baking soda. Pour mixture over crackers and spread with spatula so all crackers are covered. Bake in preheated 375 degree oven for 10 minutes. Remove from oven and sprinkle with chocolate chips. When chips have softened, spread to cover crackers. Sprinkle with nuts and let cool overnight or until set. Break into pieces.

Lois Puckett, Atlanta, GA

Chocolate Chip Rum Cake

1   18¼-ounce box yellow cake mix (without pudding)
1   3.9-ounce box instant chocolate pudding
4   eggs
1   tablespoon vanilla extract
¼   cup plus 1 tablespoon rum, divided
½   cup vegetable oil
1   cup sour cream
1   cup chopped walnuts
1   12-ounce package semisweet chocolate chips
½   cup unsalted butter
1   cup sugar
¼   cup water

In large bowl, combine cake mix and pudding mix, mixing to break up any lumps. In a medium bowl, beat eggs, vanilla and 1 tablespoon rum. Add oil and blend; mix in sour cream and blend well. Add this mixture to dry mixture, stirring only until blended. Add nuts and chocolate chips. Pour into greased 12 cup Bundt pan and bake in preheated 350 degree oven for 50 to 60 minutes, until cake tester comes out clean. Put cake, in pan, on cooling rack. Combine butter, sugar, remaining rum and water in saucepan and cook over medium heat until butter and sugar have dissolved. Poke holes in cake and pour glaze over cake while still hot. Allow 5 minutes more to cool and then turn cake out of pan. Once cake has cooled, dust with powdered sugar.

Mary Sue Howard, Atlanta, GA

Chocolate Ganache Cake

Cake

½	cup butter
1	cup sugar
4	large eggs
1	16-ounce can chocolate syrup
1	tablespoon vanilla extract
1	cup flour

Icing

½	cup heavy cream
1	cup semisweet chocolate chips

To prepare cake, cream butter and sugar until fluffy. Add eggs, one at a time. Mix in chocolate syrup and vanilla. Add flour and mix only until combined. Pour into buttered and floured 8 inch cake pan and bake in preheated 325 degree oven for 40 to 45 minutes. Center of cake should not be loose. Remove from pan and cool. To prepare icing, melt chocolate chips with cream over double boiler. Ice cooled cake.

Janet Sunshine, Atlanta, GA

Coconut Cake

Cake

1	18¼-ounce box white cake mix
	coconut milk

Frosting

2	8-ounce packages cream cheese, softened
3½	cups powdered sugar
1	teaspoon vanilla extract
1	cup unsalted butter, softened
2	6-ounce packages shredded coconut, divided

Prepare cake according to directions on box, substituting coconut milk for water. Bake in two 9 inch cake pans. Cool and slice each cake in half making four layers. To prepare frosting, beat together cream cheese, powdered sugar, vanilla and butter until light and fluffy, about 5 minutes. Mix in ¾ coconut, reserving ¼ coconut to toast for garnish. Frost cooled cake and garnish with toasted coconut.

Liz Anderson, Atlanta, GA

CHOCOLATE SURPRISE CAKE

1 18¼-ounce box dark chocolate cake mix

1 3.9-ounce package instant chocolate pudding

2 cups sour cream

3 eggs, slightly beaten

⅓ cup vegetable oil

½ cup coffee flavored liqueur

2 cups semisweet chocolate chips

Combine cake mix, pudding, sour cream, eggs, oil and liqueur; beat well. Fold in chocolate chips. Pour into greased and floured 10 inch Bundt pan and bake in preheated 350 degree oven for 1 hour.

Lynne Yancey, Atlanta, GA

Coffee Crunch Cake

1½   cups sugar
¼   cup strong coffee
¼   cup light corn syrup
1   tablespoon baking soda
1   cup whipping cream, whipped
1   8-ounce angel food cake

Combine sugar, coffee and corn syrup in saucepan that is at least 5 inches deep. Bring to boil and cook until mixture reaches 310 degrees on candy thermometer or hard-crack stage (when small amount dropped into cold water breaks with brittle snap). Press soda through sieve to remove lumps. Remove syrup from heat. Immediately add soda and stir vigorously just until mixture thickens and pulls away from sides of pan. Mixture foams rapidly when soda is added. Do not destroy foam by beating excessively. Immediately pour foamy mass into ungreased 9 inch square metal pan. Do not spread or stir. Let stand, without moving, until cool. When ready to garnish cake, knock out of pan and crush between sheets of wax paper with rolling pin to form coarse crumbs. Frost cake with whipped cream. Cover frosted cake generously and thoroughly with crushed topping. Refrigerate until ready to serve.

Jean Crichton, Burlingame, CA

Cream Cheese Peach Pound Cake

1   8-ounce package cream cheese, softened
1½   cups butter, softened
3   cups sugar
3   cups flour
1   teaspoon salt
6   eggs
1   teaspoon lemon extract
1   teaspoon vanilla extract
1   teaspoon almond extract
¼   cup peach brandy

Have all ingredients at room temperature. Cream together cream cheese and butter until smooth and fluffy; add sugar and mix until light and fluffy. Mix together flour and salt; set aside. Alternately add eggs and flour, ending with flour, creaming well after each addition. Add lemon, vanilla and almond extracts and brandy, stirring to mix well. Spoon batter into greased and floured tube pan and bake in preheated 350 degree oven for 1½ hours.

Serves 12

May be frozen after baking.

Rena Morrison, Atlanta, GA

To use whipped cream in a frosting for a cake or jelly-roll that will be refrigerated several hours or overnight, use a small amount of gelatin in the whipped cream to keep it firm. Dissolve 1 teaspoon unflavored gelatin in ¼ cup cold water; cook over low heat to dissolve. Cool to room temperature. Fold into 1 cup whipping cream, whipped. This will be sufficient to frost a two layer 9 inch cake. To make chocolate whipped cream, add 2 tablespoons powdered sugar and 2 tablespoons cocoa to 1 cup whipping cream. Refrigerate 30 minutes before whipping. To make mocha flavored whipped cream, add 1 tablespoon instant coffee along with cocoa. After cream is whipped, fold in ½ teaspoon vanilla.

Serves 10 to 12

Jean Crichton,
Burlingame, CA

Cream Cheese Chocolate Chip Cake

½	cup butter
1	8-ounce package cream cheese
1¼	cups sugar
2	eggs
2	cups flour
¼	teaspoon baking soda
¼	teaspoon salt
¼	teaspoon baking powder
¼	cup milk
1	teaspoon vanilla extract
1	12-ounce package mini semisweet chocolate chips
	powdered sugar for dusting

Cream together butter and cream cheese. Add sugar and mix until well blended. Add eggs, one at a time. Sift flour with soda, salt and baking powder. Add flour mixture alternately with milk to cream cheese mixture. Add vanilla and stir in chocolate chips. Pour ingredients into greased Bundt pan and bake in preheated 350 degree oven for 50 minutes. Remove from oven and let cool 4 minutes. Remove from pan and wrap hot cake in heavy duty aluminum foil. Serve when cool. Dust with powdered sugar.

This cake looks pretty when garnished around the bottom with chocolate dipped strawberries.

Freezes well.

Martha Jo Katz, Atlanta, GA

Flourless Chocolate Torte

1	12-ounce package semisweet chocolate chips
1½	cups sugar
1½	cups unsalted butter
¾	cup cooled strong brewed coffee
6	eggs, slightly beaten
	powdered sugar for dusting

Melt chocolate chips, sugar and butter over low heat. Stir until smooth. Cool mixture slightly and beat in coffee. Beat in eggs and pour into greased 9 inch springform pan. Place springform pan on baking sheet and bake in preheated 350 degree oven for 35 to 45 minutes, or until middle is set. Cool and refrigerate until time to serve. Invert on serving plate and sprinkle with powdered sugar.

This torte makes a wonderful Passover dessert.

Debbie Goot, Atlanta, GA

German Chocolate Apple Cake

4	apples, peeled
3	tablespoons rum
1	cup butter
2¼	cups sugar
4	eggs
2	cups flour
1	tablespoon baking powder
2	teaspoons dark cocoa
2	teaspoons cinnamon
1	teaspoon vanilla extract
¾	cup ground hazelnuts
4	squares bittersweet chocolate

Thirty minutes before preparing dough, cut apples into small pieces and soak in rum. Cream butter and sugar; add eggs and beat until well combined. Add flour, baking powder, cocoa, cinnamon, vanilla and hazelnuts; beat until blended. Carefully fold in apples and rum. Pour into greased springform pan and bake in preheated 375 degree oven for 40 to 50 minutes until tester comes out clean. Melt chocolate and pour over cake.

Jutta Putter, Germany

Lemon Pound Cake

1	cup butter, softened
½	cup shortening
3	cups sugar
3	cups flour
½	teaspoon baking powder
½	teaspoon salt
6	eggs
1	cup milk
1	teaspoon vanilla extract
2	teaspoons lemon extract

Cream together butter, shortening and sugar. Sift flour, baking powder and salt together 4 times. Add eggs, one at a time, beating well after each addition. Add flour mixture alternately with milk, beating well after each addition, beginning and ending with flour. Stir in vanilla and lemon extracts. Pour into greased and floured tube pan and bake in preheated 325 degree oven for 1¼ hours.

A glaze of fresh lemon juice and powdered sugar can be made to desired consistency and poured over warm cake.

Jerry Gaines, Anderson, SC

Oatmeal Cake

Cake

1¼	cups boiling water
1	cup rolled oats
½	cup margarine
1	cup brown sugar
1	cup sugar
2	eggs
1	teaspoon vanilla extract
1⅓	cups flour
1	teaspoon baking soda
½	teaspoon salt
1	teaspoon cinnamon

Topping

½	cup butter
1	cup brown sugar
1	egg
1	cup shredded coconut
1	cup chopped nuts

To prepare cake, pour boiling water over oats; let stand. Cream together margarine, brown sugar and sugar; add eggs and vanilla and blend thoroughly. Sift together flour, soda, salt and cinnamon. Add flour mixture to butter mixture and mix well. Mix in oats and pour into greased 9x13 inch pan and bake in preheated 350 degree oven for 25 minutes. To prepare topping, melt butter and stir in brown sugar, egg, coconut and nuts. Mix well and pour over cake. Return to oven to brown coconut.

Pauline Willis, Atlanta, GA

Pumpkin Pie Cake

2	15-ounce cans pumpkin
1	cup sugar
1½	cups evaporated milk
3	eggs
¼	teaspoon ground nutmeg
¼	teaspoon ground cloves
¼	teaspoon ground allspice
1	teaspoon ground cinnamon
1	teaspoon ground ginger (optional)
1	18.5-ounce package yellow cake mix
½	cup butter or margarine, melted

In large bowl mix at low speed pumpkin, sugar, milk, eggs, nutmeg, cloves, allspice, cinnamon and ginger until well combined, about 2 minutes. Pour mixture into greased 9x13 inch pan. Sprinkle dry cake mix over pumpkin mixture. Do not mix in. Drizzle with melted butter and bake in preheated 375 degree oven for 45 to 50 minutes. Cool for 15 minutes in pan. Cut into squares and serve with whipped cream or ice cream, if desired.

Serves 12

Spiced Pear Cake

1	29-ounce can pear halves
1	18¼-ounce box carrot or spice cake mix
¾	cup water
3	eggs
⅓	cup vegetable oil
2	teaspoons ground ginger
½	teaspoon salt
½	cup chopped walnuts or pecans
½	cup sifted powdered sugar

Drain pears, pat dry and coarsely chop. Combine cake mix, water, eggs, oil, ginger and salt. Stir until smooth. Add nuts and pears and stir gently. Pour into greased 10 inch Bundt pan and bake in preheated 350 degree oven for 40 minutes, until toothpick inserted in center comes out clean. Cool in pan on wire rack for 15 minutes. Invert on rack, remove pan and cool completely. Dust with powdered sugar before serving.

Refrigerate briefly for easier cutting.

Mary Kay Howard, Marietta, GA

Texts Cake

Cake

2	cups sugar
2	cups flour
½	cup margarine
½	cup vegetable oil
¼	cup cocoa powder
1	cup water
1	teaspoon baking soda
1	teaspoon vanilla extract
2	eggs, slightly beaten
½	cup buttermilk

Icing

½	cup margarine
¼	cup cocoa powder
⅓	cup milk
¼	teaspoon vanilla extract
1	box powdered sugar
½	cup chopped pecans or walnuts

To prepare cake, sift together sugar and flour and set aside. In saucepan, bring margarine, oil, cocoa powder and water to rapid boil but do not let it cook. Pour hot liquid over sugar and flour and stir with wire whisk. Add soda, vanilla, eggs and buttermilk. Whisk together well. Place in greased jelly-roll pan and bake in preheated 400 degree oven for 20 minutes. Ice cake immediately. To prepare icing, put margarine, cocoa powder, milk and vanilla in saucepan and cook rapidly but do not boil. Remove from heat; add powdered sugar and nuts and pour over hot cake.

Midge Tracy, Atlanta, GA

Similar recipe contributed by Erinn Tatom, Mesa, AZ

Tres Leches Cake

Cake

1	cup sugar, divided
5	eggs, separated
⅓	cup milk
¾	teaspoon vanilla extract
1	cup flour
1½	teaspoons baking powder
¼	teaspoon cream of tartar

Milk Syrup

1	12-ounce can evaporated milk
1	cup sweetened condensed milk
1	cup heavy cream
1	teaspoon vanilla extract
1	tablespoon rum

Meringue

⅔	cup sugar, divided
½	teaspoon cream of tartar, divided
⅓	cup water
2	egg whites

To prepare cake, beat ¾ cup sugar and egg yolks until light and fluffy. Stir in milk, vanilla, flour and baking powder. Beat egg whites to soft peaks, adding cream of tarter after 20 seconds. Gradually add remaining sugar and continue beating until whites are glossy and firm. Gently fold whites into yolk mixture. Spoon batter into 9x13 inch greased baking dish. Bake the cake in preheated 350 degree oven for 40 to 50 minutes or until firm and inserted toothpick comes out clean. Let cake cool completely, about 2 hours, and unmold. Replace cake in cleaned pan. Pierce all over with fork. To prepare milk syrup, combine evaporated milk, sweetened condensed milk, cream, vanilla and rum and whisk until mixed. Pour syrup slowly and evenly over cake. To prepare meringue, place all but 1 tablespoon sugar in heavy saucepan with ¼ teaspoon cream of tartar and water. Cover and cook over high heat for 2 minutes. Uncover pan and cook sugar to soft-ball stage, 239 degrees on candy thermometer. Meanwhile, beat egg whites to soft peaks with remaining cream of tartar. Add remaining sugar and continue beating to stiff peaks. Pour boiling sugar syrup in thin stream into whites and continue beating until mixture is cool. Thickly spread top of the cake with meringue, using wet spatula. Refrigerate cake for at least 2 hours before serving.

Serves 10

This is a traditional Costa Rican recipe.

Neville Pearson, Atlanta, GA

Upside-Down Berry Cakes

¼	cup flour
¼	cup sugar
½	teaspoon baking powder
	dash of salt
¼	cup milk
4	teaspoons butter, melted
1	cup fresh blueberries

Combine flour, sugar, baking powder and salt in small bowl; mix well. Add milk and butter, stirring just until flour mixture is moist. Divide batter evenly between two greased 10 ounce custard cups. Top each with ½ cup blueberries. Bake in preheated 375 degree oven for 35 minutes or until lightly browned and fruit topping is bubbly.

Serves 2

To make this dessert a lighter fare, substitute skim milk and reduced calorie stick margarine for milk and butter.

Debbie Goot, Atlanta, GA

Whipping Cream Pound Cake

3	cups sugar
1	cup butter
6	eggs
3	cups flour
1	cup whipping cream
1	teaspoon vanilla extract

Cream sugar and butter; add eggs, one at a time, beating well. Add flour alternately with cream, ending with cream; add vanilla. Pour into greased and floured tube or Bundt pan and place in cold oven; turn oven to 300 degrees and bake 1 hour 20 minutes.

Alana Shepherd, Atlanta, GA

Similar recipe submitted by Margaret Bethea, Atlanta, GA

Potpourri

HOSPITALITY

Bourbon Balls

1	cup finely chopped pecans
3	tablespoons bourbon
1	16-ounce package powdered sugar
½	cup butter, softened
1	12-ounce package semisweet chocolate chips
½	cup peanut butter chips
1	tablespoon vegetable shortening

Combine pecans and bourbon and set aside for 15 minutes. Cream sugar and butter. Add pecan/bourbon mixture and mix well. Roll into 1 inch balls and place on baking sheet lined with wax paper. Refrigerate for about 30 minutes or until well chilled. Melt chocolate, peanut butter chips and shortening in top of double boiler over simmering water. Using wooden toothpick inserted into ball, dip into melted chocolate/peanut butter, coating well. Place back on baking sheet and chill until firm. Store in airtight container.

Makes 5 dozen

David Lundy, Atlanta, GA

English Toffee

1	6-ounce package sliced almonds, divided
1	cup butter
1	cup sugar
	dash of salt
1	tablespoon water
1	tablespoon white corn syrup
1	6-ounce package semisweet chocolate chips

Toast almonds; crush half and set aside. Heat butter, sugar, salt, water and corn syrup over medium heat. Stir constantly until mixture comes to boil. After 5 minutes, stir in remaining uncrushed almonds. Do not stir what accumulates on sides of pan. Stir constantly until mixture reaches 290 degrees, hard-crack stage, on candy thermometer. Turn out toffee onto buttered jelly-roll pan or marble slab. Spread thin. Immediately spread chocolate chips over toffee; as they melt, spread to edges of candy. Cover with thin layer of crushed almonds. Cool. Break into pieces and store in airtight container.

Dorothy Thrower, Tyler, TX

Don't discard orange, grapefruit or lemon peels. Freeze them for grating or for recipes calling for zest. Also, slice peels thinly for making candied rind.

CANDIED ORANGE PEEL

2 large oranges
or 1½ grapefruits
8½ cups water, divided
½ cup sugar
1 tablespoon
white corn syrup
sugar to coat

Cut orange peels into desired shapes and combine with 8 cups water in heavy pan. Boil 5 minutes. Rinse in cold water. Repeat process, rinsing each time for 3 times. The 4th time boil peel 15 minutes. Rinse in cold water and drain well. Make syrup of sugar, corn syrup and remaining water. Cook down and add peel. Cook 10 minutes or until syrup is gone. Drain well. Place peel in bag of sugar and shake to coat. Place on wax paper until dry.

Dorothy Thrower,
Tyler, TX

Foolproof Chocolate Fudge

1   12-ounce package semisweet chocolate chips
1   6-ounce package unsweetened chocolate
     dash of salt
1   cup chopped pecans
1½ teaspoons vanilla extract

Melt chocolate chips, unsweetened chocolate and salt in double boiler or in microwave; add pecans and vanilla. Pour into 8 inch square pan lined with aluminum foil. Cool, remove from pan, peel off foil and cut into squares.

Do not double recipe. This recipe is not overly sweet.

Pecans are better if toasted.

Maryann Busby, Atlanta, GA

MEME'S PEANUT
BUTTER FUDGE

2 cups sugar

3 tablespoons
white corn syrup

1 cup heavy cream

3 tablespoons
peanut butter

¼ cup butter

1 teaspoon
vanilla extract

Heat sugar, corn syrup
and cream to soft-ball
stage. Remove from
heat and add peanut
butter, butter and vanilla.
Combine quickly and
pour into buttered
8x8 inch dish. Let set
and cut into squares.

Ansley Conner,
Atlanta, GA

My Mom's Never Fail Fudge

2¼ cups sugar
¾   cup evaporated milk
16   large marshmallows
½   cup butter
¼   teaspoon salt
1   6-ounce package semisweet chocolate chips
1   teaspoon vanilla extract
1   cup chopped pecans (optional)

Put sugar, milk, marshmallows, butter and salt into heavy saucepan. Stir constantly on low heat and bring to boil. Boil 5 minutes, stirring constantly. Remove from heat and stir in chocolate chips, vanilla and pecans, if using. Pour into greased pan. Let cool and cut into squares.

Ginny Wolf, Atlanta, GA

Granola

3	cups rolled oats
½	cup chopped walnuts
½	cup chopped pecans
1	cup cashews
1	cup shredded sweet coconut
1	teaspoon cinnamon
½	teaspoon nutmeg
⅓	cup dark brown sugar
¼	cup plus 3 tablespoons maple syrup
¼	cup vegetable oil
¾	teaspoon salt
½	cup raisins
½	cup chopped dates
1	teaspoon sugar

In large bowl, combine oats, walnuts, pecans, cashews, coconut, cinnamon, nutmeg and brown sugar. Mix well with hands, coating everything evenly. In separate bowl, combine maple syrup, oil and salt. Mix well with whisk. Combine both mixtures and spread onto 2 baking sheets or 2 jelly-roll pans. Put pans side by side on same rack in oven. Bake in preheated 250 degree oven for 60 minutes, switching pans left to right and stirring evenly every 15 minutes to ensure even browning. Put raisins and dates in large bowl and sprinkle with sugar, separating raisins and coating everything evenly. Remove granola from oven and transfer back into large bowl. Mix everything together and place in airtight container for storage.

This recipe is easily customized. It's a great way to get kids to experiment in the kitchen. Honey or molasses can be used in place of maple syrup. Other dried fruit can be used in place of raisins and dates. Just have fun mixing and matching, but keep amounts similar.

David Lundy, Atlanta, GA

STRAW STACKS

1 12-ounce package butterscotch chips

1 5-ounce can Chinese noodles

1 12-ounce can cocktail peanuts

Melt chips in double boiler. Add noodles and peanuts. Mix well. Drop by teaspoonfuls on wax paper.

Makes 45 to 50 stacks

"You can never eat just one straw stack. We have to make these every Thanksgiving or Christmas. We share them with company and friends. You could use other flavors of chips, but butterscotch is a family favorite."

Bobbie Kirkland, Ball Ground, GA

Sweet Garlic Pickles

1	46-ounce jar whole dill pickles (not kosher dills)
4	garlic cloves
3	tablespoons pickling spices in cheesecloth
3	cinnamon sticks
1	cup apple cider vinegar
3	cups sugar

Slice pickles into ¼ inch slices. Rinse well in cold water. Drain and pack back into rinsed jar with garlic, spices and cinnamon sticks. Warm vinegar and sugar until dissolved, stirring continuously; pour over pickles until covered. Replace lid tightly and place jar upside down in refrigerator for 2 weeks. Turn upright and enjoy.

These pickles will keep indefinitely and are great for gifts.

Maryann Busby, Atlanta, GA

Mama Mia's Pasta Sauce

1	garlic clove
1	onion, chopped
3	tablespoons olive oil
1	pound ground pork
1	pound ground beef
1	pound (country style) pork ribs
2	15-ounce cans tomato sauce
2	29-ounce cans tomato purée
2	28-ounce cans chopped tomatoes
1	6-ounce can tomato paste
3	bay leaves
	salt and pepper to taste
	pasta

In large saucepan sauté garlic and onion in olive oil until tender. Add pork, beef and ribs and cook until brown, stirring every few minutes. After meat is brown, drain off extra fat. Reduce heat to low or simmer; add tomato sauce, tomato purée, tomatoes, tomato paste, bay leaves, salt and pepper. Stir well, cover pot with lid and cook 3 to 4 hours, stirring often. Turn off heat and let remain sitting on burner for ½ hour. Remove bones from ribs. Cook pasta and drain water. Remove bay leaves and pour sauce over pasta.

This sauce freezes well.

Sharon Lufkin, Jonesboro, GA

SPEEDY SPICED PEACHES

2 16-ounce cans cling peach halves

whole cloves

1 cup peach syrup drained from peaches

½ cup cider vinegar

3-4 cinnamon sticks, broken in half

½ cup sugar

A week or 10 days ahead, stud each peach half with 3 or 4 whole cloves and store in refrigerator. When ready to prepare, heat peach syrup, vinegar, cinnamon sticks and sugar. Add peaches and simmer for several minutes; cool. Remove cinnamon sticks and discard. Store peaches in refrigerator. When ready to serve, remove cloves, drain and place on chilled lettuce leaves or in glass bowl.

Margaret Bethea, Atlanta, GA

Sausage and Peppers Sauce

2   pounds sweet Italian sausage links
3   tablespoons olive oil
1   cup finely chopped onion
3   red peppers, stemmed, seeds removed, cut into medium size julienne
1   cup red wine
1   2¼-pound can plum tomatoes, including liquid
1   cup water
1   tablespoon oregano
1   teaspoon thyme
     salt and pepper to taste
1   teaspoon red pepper flakes
1   teaspoon fennel seeds
½   cup chopped Italian parsley
6   garlic cloves, finely chopped
     cooked pasta

Pierce sausage links with fork and put in pot with ½ inch water. Place pot over medium heat and simmer uncovered for about 20 minutes. Eventually the pot will boil dry and sausages will begin to fry in their own fat. Turn them occasionally and cook for 20 minutes more, or until well browned. Remove from pan and set aside. Pour fat out but do not wash pot. Over low heat add olive oil and onion, cover and cook about 25 minutes, or until tender. Add red pepper, increase heat and cook uncovered for 5 minutes, stirring often. Add wine, tomatoes, water, oregano, thyme, salt, pepper and red pepper flakes. Bring to boil, reduce heat and simmer partially covered for 30 minutes. Slice sausage and add to sauce. Add fennel and simmer uncovered for 20 minutes. Add parsley and garlic and simmer for 5 minutes. Serve over pasta.

Loredana Reuter, Cumming, GA

EASY BLENDED HOLLANDAISE SAUCE

egg yolks, room temperature
1½ tablespoons lemon juice
¾ cup butter
cayenne pepper (optional)

Combine egg yolks and lemon juice in blender. Melt butter and heat until it bubbles, being careful not to brown. Turn blender on high speed and immediately pour in hot butter in slow, steady stream. Whirl until well blended. Turn off blender and serve. For added flavor add dash cayenne after butter is incorporated. Whirl for 30 seconds and serve.

Hallie Henrickson, Douglasville, GA

HOSPITALITY

Index

HOSPITALITY

INDEX

HOSPITALITY

INDEX

INDEX

INDEX

INDEX

Conversions

pinch or dash = less than ⅛ teaspoon

1 tablespoon = ½ fluid ounce

2 tablespoons = 1 fluid ounce

3 teaspoons = 1 tablespoon

4 tablespoons = ¼ cup

16 tablespoons = 1 cup

2 cups = 1 pint

2 pints = 1 quart

4 quarts = 1 gallon

8 quarts = 1 peck

4 pecks = 1 bushel

#1 can = 2 cups

#2 can = 2½ cups

#3 can = 4 cups

#10 can = 12-13 cups

Equivalents

Asparagus: 1 pound = 12-20 spears

Bacon: 1 slice bacon = 1 tablespoon crumbled

Bell pepper: 1 large = 1 cup chopped

Bread crumbs: 4 slices = 1 cup fine

Broccoli: 1 pound = 2 cups chopped

Butter: 1 stick = ½ cup = ¼ pound
2 sticks = 1 cup = ½ pound

Celery: 2 medium ribs = ½ cup chopped

Cheese: 4 ounces = 1 cup shredded

Chocolate: 1 square = 1 ounce
1 (12-ounce) package
morsels = 2 cups

Corn: 2 medium ears = 1 cup kernels

Garlic: 1 clove = ½ teaspoon minced

Herbs: 1 tablespoon fresh =
1 teaspoon dried

Lemon: 1 medium lemon =
3 tablespoons juice
1 medium lemon =
2-3 teaspoons zest

Nuts: 1 pound = 3½ cups chopped

Onion: 1 large onion = 1 cup chopped

Pasta: 2 ounces uncooked = 1 serving
1 cup uncooked macaroni =
2 cups cooked
1 pound spaghetti = 8 cups cooked

Peaches: 4 medium = 2½ cups sliced

Potatoes: 1 pound = 3½-4 cups chopped
1 pound = 2 cups mashed

Rice: 1 cup regular = 3 cups cooked

Shrimp: 1 pound shelled = 8 ounces meat
1 pound shelled = 2 cups mashed

Strawberries: 1 pint = 2 cups sliced

Sugar: 1 pound granulated = 2 cups
1 pound brown sugar = 2¼ cups
1 pound powdered = 4½ cups

Tomato: 1 large = 1 cup chopped

Whipping cream: 1 cup = 2 cups whipped

SUBSTITUTIONS

Baking Powder:
> 1 teaspoon = ¼ teaspoon baking soda + ½ teaspoon cream of tartar

Biscuit mix:
> 1 cup = 1 cup all-purpose flour + 1½ teaspoons baking powder +
>> 2 tablespoons shortening

Breadcrumbs:
> 1 cup = ¾ cup cracker crumbs

Broth (chicken, beef or vegetable):
> 1 cup = 1 bouilion cube or 1 teaspoon granules + 1 cup boiling water

Buttermilk:
> 1 cup = 1 cup whole milk + 2 tablespoons vinegar

Chocolate, semisweet:
> 3 squares (3 ounces) = ½ cup semi-sweet morsels

Chocolate, unsweetened:
> 1 ounce = 3 tablespoons unsweetened cocoa + 1 tablespoon butter

Cornstarch:
> 1 tablespoon = 2 tablespoons all-purpose flour for thickening

Corn Syrup (dark):
> 1 cup = ¾ cup light corn syrup + ¼ cup molasses

Flour, self-rising:
> 1 cup sifted = 1 cup sifted all-purpose + 1½ teaspoons baking powder +
>> ⅛ teaspoon salt

Garlic:
> 1 clove = ⅛ teaspoon powdered

Ginger, fresh:
> 1 teaspoon minced = ¼ teaspoon powdered

Half-and-half:
> 1 cup = ½ cup whole milk + ½ cup cream

Herbs:
> 1 teaspoon dried + 1 tablespoon fresh

Ketchup:
> ½ cup tomato sauce + 2 tablespoons sugar + 1 tablespoon vinegar

Lemon juice:
> 1 teaspoon fresh = ½ teaspoon vinegar

Milk:
> 1 cup = ½ cup evaporated + ½ cup water

Sugar, light brown:
> 1 cup = ½ cup dark brown sugar + ½ cup granulated

Sugar, granulated:
> 1 cup = 1¾ cups powdered sugar or 1 cup firmly packed light brown sugar

Tomato sauce:
> 2 cups = 1 cup tomato paste + 1 cup water

HOSPITALITY Recipes Full of Love

Shepherd Center Auxiliary
2020 Peachtree Road NW
Atlanta, GA 30309

Please send me_____copies at $24.95 EACH, plus
$6.95 shipping and handling (GEORGIA RESIDENTS
ADD 8% SALES TAX). Payable in U.S. funds. Make checks
payable to Shepherd Center Auxiliary.
Enclosed is my check or money order
in the amount of $_____

Please charge my: (circle one)   MasterCard   VISA

CARD: _____ EXP:_____

SIGNATURE: _____

NAME:_____

_____

ADDRESS: _____

_____

CITY:_____

STATE:_____ ZIP: _____

DAYTIME PHONE: _____

HOSPITALITY Recipes Full of Love

Shepherd Center Auxiliary
2020 Peachtree Road NW
Atlanta, GA 30309

Please send me_____copies at $24.95 EACH, plus
$6.95 shipping and handling (GEORGIA RESIDENTS
ADD 8% SALES TAX). Payable in U.S. funds. Make checks
payable to Shepherd Center Auxiliary.
Enclosed is my check or money order
in the amount of $_____

Please charge my: (circle one)   MasterCard   VISA

CARD: _____ EXP:_____

SIGNATURE: _____

NAME:_____

_____

ADDRESS: _____

_____

CITY:_____

STATE:_____ ZIP: _____

DAYTIME PHONE: _____

HOSPITALITY Recipes Full of Love

Shepherd Center Auxiliary
2020 Peachtree Road NW
Atlanta, GA 30309

Please send me_____copies at $24.95 EACH, plus
$6.95 shipping and handling (GEORGIA RESIDENTS
ADD 8% SALES TAX). Payable in U.S. funds. Make checks
payable to Shepherd Center Auxiliary.
Enclosed is my check or money order
in the amount of $_____

Please charge my: (circle one)   MasterCard   VISA

CARD: _____ EXP:_____

SIGNATURE: _____

NAME:_____

_____

ADDRESS: _____

_____

CITY:_____

STATE:_____ ZIP: _____

DAYTIME PHONE: _____